I GOT 99 PROBLEMS BUT A BILL AIN'T ONE

A HIP-HOPPER'S GUIDE TO ESTABLISHING
AND LEAVING A FINANCIAL LEGACY

RODNEY B. PEARSON

ISBN-13: 9780998271811 Print
ISBN-13: 9780998271828 Digital
Library of Congress Control Number 2020901763

Common Sense Learning, CANTON, MICHIGAN

MY DEDICATION

Learn from the errors of the past, to create a legacy for the future...

Writing this book has completely taken me out of my comfort zone. I have NEVER professed a love for writing, nor have I desired to be in the spotlight. This is something very new for me. What started out as an inside joke with one of my best friends, has turned into a project that I am looking to expound on and help as many people as I possibly can. The information in this book is needed, especially for my community. I do not know ALL of the answers, and I probably don't know HALF of the questions, but I have opened up my heart to give you a PORTION of the information that will allow you to establish good financial habits and begin to create a lasting financial legacy for you and your family.

I didn't really know what I was getting into when I sat down one day and started typing stuff that came into my mind. I didn't know I was actually writing a book like this...I just thought I was going to write a couple of paragraphs and post it online as a joke. But guess what – the joke was on me! I have spent hours writing this book and trying to make sure that it made sense and that anyone could understand it. I pray I have accomplished that feat! I am just so grateful to God that I have been able to actually put in writing something that He gave me in my spirit.

I would like to thank God for giving me the inspiration every step of the way. Without His guidance, I would have never been able to publish my thoughts. I would like to thank my brothers Dorian and Montie who inspired this whole thing with their financial questions. Now they can actually "buy my book" to get the answers they need. I would like to thank my other "BROTHERS" – Dooze, Cal, Johnny, Bo, Binky, Fatty, Laron, and Mondy – for always supporting a brother…no matter what. I would like to thank my ATL family – Chonda, Eric, & Malik – for all of the love they have shown me. I would like to thank my DET family – Angie, Marshall, & Parker – for always sticking by me. I would like to thank my father and his wife – Roy and Doris Pearson – for keeping me close to their hearts. I would like to thank my WONDERFUL in-laws – Anthony & Bernadine Hoston – for loving this crazy boy from EStL. I would like to thank three of the smartest, most beautiful children EVER – Alexis, Breann, and Casey (the ABC's). Daddy loves you and ALWAYS will. And finally I would like to thank my wonderful wife, Antoinette, who pushed and prodded me and kept me on track to finish what I started. I could not have done this without you!!! You all have truly been an inspiration for me and I Love You All.

THANK YOU! THANK YOU!! THANK YOU!!!

TABLE
OF
CONTENTS

TABLE OF CONTENTS

TABLE OF CONTENTS

THE FOREWORD

FOREWORD

FOREWORD

THE FOREWORD

From the moment that the doctor spanked our little bottoms, we are programmed to understand the importance of education. We are continuously taught about all of the necessary things in life. We are taught how to speak, how to walk, how to exist in a social environment, and even how to conjugate verbs or differentiate functions. Education is gaining knowledge and knowledge is awareness. We spend years learning information that is needed for us to attain a career and live what most people feel is a happy life...the "perfect" life. Usually our idea of a "perfect" life includes a spouse, children, a home, two cars, yearly vacations, a career, and working forty years until you can actually enjoy the relatively small amount of money that you may have saved... if possible.

The "perfect" life is not living... it is surviving. The road to financial freedom is necessary if we want to truly live. In this book, we will begin "Thinkin' of a Master Plan," our roadmap to understanding where we are and where we want to go as it pertains to our personal portfolios. The "Golden Rule" states "He who rules the gold makes the rules." In this book, we will study ways of making our own Golden Rule. My adaptation of the Golden Rule would say "Rod who rules his own gold, makes his own rules!" Now that my friend is living!!!

Financial freedom does not come easy and anyone that says different is not being truthful. There is very little chance that you will come across an opportunity that will allow you to gain financial freedom overnight…not impossible, just not likely. The Bible says, "The race is not given to the swift nor the strong, but he who endures until the end (Ecclesiastes 9:11)." If you design and ENACT your Master Plan, your end will result in you gaining the freedom to do all of the things in this life that you have always dreamed. We all have situations that arise in our life that cause issues. Life is filled with trials and tribulations, but if we develop our Master Plan and work the plan, we may have *99 PROBLEMS, BUT A BILL AIN'T ONE!!!*

THE FOREWORD

THE
INTRO

INTRODUCTION

THE INTRO

According to Lexico powered by Oxford Dictionary, a problem is defined as "a matter or situation regarded as unwelcomed or harmful and needing to be dealt with and overcome."[1] Everybody has problems. They could be as small as not knowing what to wear to church or as large as having to appear before a judge for some kind of offense. Problems could possibly cause physical, emotional, spiritual, or financial harm for those that are experiencing them. The key to a problem though is knowing how to deal with them and not allowing them to fester and get worse.

I remember one day sitting in my favorite chair at home, watching a little ESPN when suddenly my phone begins to ring. This was nothing unusual because my phone is known to ring about 5 times per hour… be it my wife, kids, friends or business associates. My wife calls it a hotline or as my more mature readers may understand, a party line. But for whatever reason, this particular time seemed a little different. I had yet to look at my phone, but there was pause in my mind before I picked it up to answer. I asked myself a question, "Why was this particular call any different than the other 100 calls I receive on any given day? I looked at the phone and saw a number that I did not recognize, but a prefix that was far too familiar. The call was coming from a number that had an 888 area code. Now I may not have known the name of the caller, but I definitely knew what the call was about. If you are like a lot of us, you already know what I am talking about when I discuss a call from an 888 area code. Chances are very high that this call was coming from some sort of bill collector. Would you answer the phone? Or would you do as I did and let it go to voicemail? Don't answer that question. It is only rhetorical…it doesn't require you to answer. That's mainly because I probably already *know* the answer. Everything depends on your current financial situation. If your finances are in a good position you will answer the call. But if your finances are not, you will probably let the call go to a voicemail system that will more than likely go unheard. For the former, the call is not a source of any anxiety, but for the latter, that call could be a major source of stress.

There is nothing like stressing over financial issues. Financial stress can impact almost every aspect of your life. If you are constantly worried about how much or how little money you have, how to feed and house your family, or how to keep your job, you can develop any number of stress-related illnesses. Just like any illness, if it continues to go untreated, it can become life threatening. Financial stress has also been known to break up *many* happy homes. According to a survey conducted by SunTrust Bank in 2015, 35 percent of the surveyed respondents indicated that they were experiencing relationship issues due to financial stress.[2] "Money really touches everything. It impacts people's lives," said Emmet Burns, Brand Marketing director for SunTrust. The American Psychological Association stated that at least three quarters of the American population has experienced some form of financial stress with about a quarter of the population experiencing severe financial stress.[3] As would be expected, those in the lower income brackets tend to experience higher levels of financial stress. I mean, who wouldn't be stressed when there is too much month at the end of your money? It should be everyone's goal to live life like Jay-Z. Aside from being one of the wealthiest hip-hop artists of all time, being married to a megastar like Beyoncé, and having adoring fans that span three generations, Jay-Z has zero financial stress. Since growing up in the projects of Brooklyn and struggling with his family to make ends meet, Jay-Z has amassed a net worth of over $1 billion through his many investments and Hall of Fame music career. Jay-Z may have his fair share of problems, *but money ain't one of them*!

In 2016, the Federal Reserve conducted a survey where they found that over 31 percent of the American population was struggling to take care of their most **BASIC** household living expenses.[4] That amounts to almost a third of the American population. Imagine a person standing on your left and on your right. By pure statistics, one of you will be overcome with serious financial debt and unable to provide the *simple* things needed to care for your family…MAN that hurt my manhood just writing it!!! 1 Timothy 5:8 from the King James Version of the Bible states, "But if any provide not for his own, and specially for those of his own house, he hath denied the faith, and is worse than an infidel." Everyone wants to make sure that they have food, clothing, and a place to call home. But based on the numbers provided, about one in three will not be able to provide all of these necessities for their family. But this is not that kind of book! This book is not about how forty-three percent of households with an income below $40,000 do not have a bank account. Or how only forty-four percent of all US households have life insurance. Or how fifty-five percent of all Americans do not know their credit score. This is not a book about statistics, trends, or the past. Check that! This IS a book about acknowledging the past; but it is also a book about envisioning the future. We use lessons from the past to guide our futures. Often times the hardest thing for us to do is to be personally honest about our sins, our struggles, our addictions, and our shortcomings. We live in a culture that frowns upon us admitting weakness of any kind, especially people of color. I am a 5' 6" sports fanatic that enjoys playing basketball with my boys. Our team was known as "The Family Squad." No matter the court, no matter the time, no matter the competition, we always knew we were going to win! Weakness was not allowed on our team! You can never admit any weakness in your hoop game. That is an acceptable attitude when you are a 5' 6" shooting guard on the basketball court, but not so much when you are talking about your financial health. Sometimes financially we feel like the Life Alert commercial… "I've fallen and I can't get up!" Well I'm here to tell you that we CAN get up! Chinese philosopher Lao Tzu taught us, "The journey of a thousand miles begins with one step."[5] We get up by taking that first step and continue by putting one foot in front of the other. Reading this book, that is a first step. The journey continues when we admit that we have a problem, decide that we want our financial life to change for the better, and then search for solutions that will allow us to do the things in life that make us happy. We may have had some issues in the past and fallen financially, but let us admit our mistakes and forge a plan to help us get into a position where we are secure and regain what we may have lost. I call this *Getting Back to Zero*. Once we get back to zero, it is a lot easier to achieve our goal of financial freedom.

Everyone wants to have financial freedom, but few understand the dedication and commitment it takes to actually achieve it. The Cambridge English Dictionary defines **dedication** as "the activity of giving a lot of your energy and time to something that you think is important." Dedication is needed in every aspect of our life...spiritually, physically, educationally, and financially. We exhibit this dedication easily when we worship our God, exercise our bodies, and study our classwork; however, dedication to our financial health tends to be a little more difficult. In this book, I will discuss strategies to become dedicated to your financial well-being. Everything starts with you. I can give you some of the necessary information needed to gain more freedoms, but if you don't put into action the steps needed to improve your financial health, you will fail. As my boy Hugh Williams used to say, "I'm going to give it to you straight with no chaser!" You have to *Keep It 100* with yourself. That means to keep yourself real and true, to be honest and stick to the way you are, no matter what anyone else thinks. In this book, I will discuss how you can take the information that is provided and guide your journey to financial freedom so that you can **live** life.

According to the Federal Trade Commission (FTC), over 75 percent of all credit reports contain errors, with 20 percent of all reports containing "potentially material errors."[6] In order to work our Master Plan, we must spend time on developing an excellent credit score. The Process is our way of looking at our past credit performance and establishing a plan to make sure that we develop and keep our credit score in the Excellent range. Our credit score can go a long way in determining our financial future and we must dedicate ourselves to making sure we protect it.

Another topic for discussion is the very simple concept of spending less than you earn. This is probably one of the simplest premises regarding financial freedom, but it is also the hardest to understand and the most difficult to practice in earnest. The simple rules of financial freedom can be summed up in four statements. 1) Pay your bills on time, 2) Earn more in income than you pay out, 3) Make sure you have the money available when the bills are due, and 4) Diversify your income so that if one source falters, you have other sources to stand in the gap.

Death to Debt is another topic of discussion. FUN FACT – having debt is never a good thing...NEVER! Now we all understand that debt is actually a necessary evil, but if you choose to become servants to debt, you will never gain financial freedom. If your desire is to purchase a home, most will not have the liquid assets available to purchase it outright. Same with a car and most other large purchases you desire or need. Let me say this as simple and as plain as I know how: DEBT IS NOT YOUR FRIEND!!! *Death to Debt* is a concept whereby you use credit as a last resort, not your first line of defense. Is it a necessity to purchase that home, car, or appliance at this very moment? Are there alternatives to achieve the same desired goal?

When you are developing your plan for financial freedom, you must never forget to *Protect Your Neck*. What good does it do you to build up your personal portfolio only to have it taken away in an instant? According to the Bureau of Justice Statistics, "the aggregate number of newly filed, reopened, and reactivated court cases reported to the Court Statistics Project (CSP) from the nation's state courts reached a record high 102.4 million incoming cases in 2006."[7] Over 15 million of these cases are civil lawsuits. The annual cost to the US economy for litigation is over $239 BILLION...that is billion with a "B". That is a source on some else's 10 list but a possible large debt to you. Because of our society's penchant for litigation, you must always be mindful of that fact and find different ways of protecting your portfolio.

As someone that has grown up in a capitalistic society, I love "toys" just like everyone else. I want the big house with a five-car garage, cars to fill up the spaces, a motorcycle, a jet ski, and all of the newest electronics on the market. I live for the toys! But other than the big house, which one of these toys is actually an asset that will make me money? If your goal is to truly be financially free, you must resist making purchases that go against this premise. If you spend as much of your time creating wealth as possible, you will be able to enjoy even bigger toys. As I speak with different people looking to gain some form of freedom, I always ask the question "What is your carrot?" When I was younger, I used to watch a Bugs Bunny cartoon titled "The Grey Hounded Hare." In this cartoon, a mechanical rabbit starts to circle a racetrack and the greyhounds immediately follow. They run faster and faster to try to catch the rabbit. They keep chasing the rabbit, but they can never catch it. Did you miss that??? The greyhounds keep chasing! They have run this race hundreds of times before and know that they will not catch the rabbit, but they keep chasing. They are dedicated and determined to reach the goal of catching that rabbit. It is like a carrot dangling in front of their face. You also need to have your dangling carrot. You need a goal that you are continuously chasing. You need to have the determination and dedication of those greyhounds and continue running toward your goal of financial freedom. As Dr. Benjamin E. Mays said, "The tragedy of life does not lie in not reaching your goal. The tragedy lies in not having a goal to reach."[8]

Killing your debt and resisting the temptation of overspending can only go so far. In order to truly gain financial freedom, you must concentrate your efforts on increasing your income. I will discuss the concept of "The 10" and the different types of income streams you can develop to achieve that goal a little later in this book. To become truly financially free, passive income is a must. Passive income is income resulting from cash flow generated on a regular basis requiring minimal or no effort on your part. There are several different types of passive income and I will discuss many of them in this book. I also want everyone to stop aspiring to become rich. Being rich just means you have money at the present moment. The goal should not be to become rich, but to become wealthy. A wealthy person has sustainable assets...a legacy. Wealth is measured in time, not dollars. Your portfolio is as important, if not more important, than anything in your life. Everyone has a portfolio, both large and small. The question is how well will you maintain your portfolio? By reading this book, you will learn the importance of a healthy portfolio and begin the journey of protecting, nurturing, and cultivating it.

Benjamin Parker, the uncle of our favorite web slinger Spiderman, told us "With great power comes great responsibility." This is so true when it comes to financial knowledge. Once you have read this book and developed your Master Plan, you will be tooled with great

power. My goal is to start you on the road to financial freedom so that

through your philanthropic works, you can help someone else get started

on his or her journey as well. In other words, pass it on.

Are you ready to take that next step? Then in the immortal

words of the great poet M.C. Hammer... *Let's Get It Started*!!!

If you want to change your direction
If your time of life is at hand
Well don't be the rule, be the exception
A good way to start is to stand
Put one foot in front of the other
And soon you'll be walking 'cross the floor
Put one foot in front of the other
And soon you'll be walking out the door

"Put One Foot in Front of the Other" by
Mickey Rooney & Keenan Wynn

THINKIN'
OF A
MASTER

PLAN

CHAPTER ONE

CHAPTER 1 – THINKIN' OF A MASTER PLAN

I remember 1987 as if it were yesterday. I said goodbye to a lot of friends as I graduated from the greatest high school in the country and moved into what I thought was adulthood. I watched as Dutch and his team of commandos hunted a *Predator,* Murtaugh and Riggs combined to form a *Lethal Weapon,* and Gordon Gekko reminded us that "Greed, for lack of a better word, is Good" on *Wall Street.* I made sure I was home watching Cliff and Claire raise their children on *The Cosby Show,* the patrons of the bar calling Norm as he walked into *Cheers,* and Dorothy, Rose, Blanche, and Sophia owning Miami on *The Golden Girls.* Those were memories of wonderful times, simpler times. Times when debt was something I had no knowledge and didn't even attempt to think about. In 1987, I also developed a huge love of Hip-Hop. My friend Darryl and I visited the record store every Tuesday trying to find the next up and coming Hip-Hop artist. We were treasure hunters looking for our next bounty each time we entered the store. Then it happened. I picked up an album from a MC/DJ duo from Long

Island, NY and was instantly transformed into a Hip-Hop junkie. The classic album *Paid In Full* by Eric B. and Rakim molded me during a period of time when Hip-Hop was still in its relative infancy. It had only been 8 years since the Sugar Hill Gang began popularizing the Hip-Hop genre with the classic anthem "Rapper's Delight" when Eric B. and Rakim came along and took the rap game to a whole new level. The flow of the lyrics from Rakim and the hardness of the beats from Eric B. still resonate today. Rakim has been widely considered one of the best, if not THE best, lyricist ever. Now I am not trying to turn this book into a history lesson on Hip-Hop, but homage is due when you are referring to greatness, and Eric B. and Rakim were great. The title track from the *Paid In Full* album gave us these lyrics:

> *Thinkin' of a master plan*
> *Cuz ain't nothing but sweat inside my hand.*
> *So I dig into my pocket, all my money is spent*
> *So I dig deeper but still comin' up with lint.*

Merriam-Webster says a "Master Plan" is a detailed plan for doing something that will require a lot of time and effort.[9] A Master Plan includes analysis of a situation, recommendations for improvement, and proposals for implementation. You will be "Thinkin' of a Master

Plan" as you begin your road to financial freedom…because you too want to get rid of the lint in your pockets.

As Ben Franklin once famously said, "If you fail to plan, you are planning to fail." These words ring true in any aspect of life. In sports, determining which pitch to throw to certain hitters, choosing between a running play and a passing play, and developing the perfect lineup against the Golden State Warriors are choices that require a game plan. Even simple things require a game plan. What foods should you eat when you get a craving or how much water should you drink to flush your system are choices in dieting. Planning for your financial freedom is even more essential. As a young man growing up in a very impoverished city, the subjects of wealth and financial legacy were never stressed, let alone talked about in my neighborhood. For whatever reason, a large portion of the Black community has not made financial planning a family rule like going to school, going to church, or getting a job. We have been very lackadaisical in our dissemination of the *basic* economic knowledge to our own people. We all want the finer things in life for our children. We want them to have a better life than we did. However, in the Black community we have failed when it comes to preparing our children for life in this capitalistic society. That is why I have stepped out of my comfort zone and written this book. I am not an author, nor do I pretend to play one on television. This is just my way of getting people to think about a subject that we all should be well versed and try to help change this cycle of "unreadiness" among all people, but with a special emphasis on my community.

As a man of color, I find it very unnerving that the important concepts of wealth building and financial legacy were not, or rather ARE not being emphasized as much as they should be within our community. This is not because of a lack of knowledge, but rather an innate characteristic of our community to hold on to information for a sentiment that someone may one day take it away. The stereotypical idea of crabs in a barrel is alive and present when it comes to this idea of financial legacy. Now I will not go much deeper into that subject in THIS book, but rather I ask that you turn your mind to reflect on the strategies that should be used to build a legacy and create wealth for all of my brothers and sisters. The past is the past and you cannot change that, but you can redirect your present towards a path of financial freedom and begin to create a legacy for you and your future generations.

We have survived in this country for almost 400 years, but let's stop surviving and start living! As Maya Angelou was quoted saying, "Do the best you can until you know better. Then when you know better, do better."[10] You started down the path of knowing better by reading this book. Now is the time to do better by developing a Master Plan that you will use to create wealth and create a legacy.

DEDICATION, COMMITMENT, & DETERMINATION

> *Keep your dreams alive. Understand to achieve anything requires faith and belief in yourself, vision, hard work, determination, and dedication. Remember all things are possible for those who believe.*[11]

2-time 100-meter Olympic Gold Medalist Gail Devers

These words ring so true when you considering your Master Plan for a financial legacy. First and foremost, you must believe in yourself. Nothing will be accomplished if you do not believe that you will accomplish it. You must understand that the road to a financial legacy requires dedication, commitment, and determination. Dedicate yourself to the notion that you want to live a life with less stress and more enjoyment, while at the same time understanding that nothing worth fighting for is going to be easy. Our ancestors taught us that freedom has never been free and financial freedom is no different. You are bound to have some financial peaks and valleys, but if you remain dedicated to the plan, you will be better prepared to overcome them. The commitment portion of the plan is usually the hardest. To commit one's self is to be loyal. In this case, being loyal is to the plan of financial freedom, the development of a legacy of wealth, and all that comes along with this quest. The plan will only work if you believe in its purpose, its direction, and its outcome. To achieve this commitment, you must be true to yourself. For those of you that are starting off as I did with serious financial flaws, you must acknowledge the fact that your financial portfolio is not as secure as you would like it to be. Admit that you need help in reaching your goals and commit your efforts to creating a Master Plan to "Live" and not "Survive." Let's begin by speaking these words aloud:

> I <u>RESIST</u> the temptation of my inactions.
> I <u>SUBMIT</u> myself to the fact of not knowing.
> I <u>ADMIT</u> to myself that I can do better.
> I <u>COMMIT</u> myself to the task of improving.

The more that you speak these words into the atmosphere, the more you will begin to believe them, and most importantly, *LIVE* them. One of the greatest lyricists ever, Eminem, said these lines: *"If you had one shot or one opportunity to seize everything you ever wanted in one moment, would you capture or just let it slip away?"* We all only get one life…why not make the most of it?

My father is a Math professor, who for 45 years and counting, has worked every day of his adult life teaching a subject that he absolutely loves. Growing up in East St. Louis, Illinois, he was and still is my idol. He was always there to take me, my sister, and even my friends on family vacations, to help me whenever necessary, and to provide the things in life that I thought I needed. Even though I grew up in a very impoverished community, I didn't really realize it. I never felt deprived of anything. But my father, as great as he is, was like so many in my community – he worked to survive. Survival is predicated on enduring even in the midst of difficult circumstances. Survival requires doing the things necessary even when it may seem too difficult. Survival is a means to an end, a continuation of existence. My father survived…he endured…but he did not live! He always provided for us an environment that was safe and secure, one that I will forever be grateful. I can only imagine how much better our relationship would have been had some of his time spent working, had been spent enjoying family a little more. Those are regrets…the kind of which I no longer want to experience. I have three beautiful daughters and I have dedicated myself to creating enough wealth that would allow them to live life for generations. For me, the time for survival has passed. The time for living…well that's right now.

MASTER PLAN DEVELOPMENT

According to the New York Federal Reserve as composed by Debt.org, Americans were on pace to surpass $13.86 TRILLION in debt in the third quarter of 2018.[12] Almost $4 trillion of this debt is non-mortgage debt meaning credit cards, auto loans, student loans and personal loans. That would be 17 consecutive quarters where the consumer debt figure has increased. Consider these facts from Debt.org:

- More than 189 million Americans have credit card debt.
- The average credit card holder has at least four cards.
- The average amount of credit card debt owed by the cardholder is $8,398.
- There have been about 1.6 million bankruptcy filings since 2018.

- An average of 1 million homes enter foreclosure each year since 2017.
- The mortgage delinquency rate is 7.58% since 2012.[16]

Can you see the problem in these numbers? This is telling me that there are a large number of people having financial issues.

The goal of this book is to provide a "Blueprint" for everyone – those who are financially established and ready to improve on their legacy and those who have made previous financial mistakes and are looking for some redirection and some guidance. As with any issue or condition, the first step to recovery is admitting that you actually have a problem. If you don't admit that you have a problem, you will continue to run in place and do the same types of things that got you into that *messed up* position in the first place. Without admitting your problems, your financial problems may continue to fester and grow even larger. Admit your problem and learn from it. How do you learn from your admission? You learn by discovering the reason or reasons that allowed you to get into this situation in the first place and instituting steps to prevent it from occurring again in the future. Was it because of a job layoff? Solution – create your own jobs. Maybe it was because of a medical emergency that caused large medical expenses. Solution – invest in insurance protections. Often times it is just plain old overspending that caused us to create the massive amounts of debt that we deal with daily. Solution – create a budget and follow it. Whatever the cause, understand it and develop your plan to try to prevent similar situations from happening. Some of you are reading this book because you have a problem and you know it but haven't admitted it quite yet. You are living with too much month at the end of your money and it's causing you serious pain. Debt is causing strains within your relationships and uneasiness within yourself. You know what…SKIP IT!!! Let it go! Just admit that you have a problem and let's move forward.

FOR REAL AMEX?!?!

The year of 1987 provide other memories for me that may not have been as joyous as others. For the first time in my life I was away from home and living on my own. I was making decisions that would forever change my life – some very good and some very bad. One such bad decision came via a huge misunderstanding with American Express. For the longest time, credit card companies were allowed to "post up" on college campuses and offer students the chance to apply for a credit card. More times than not, the students would be approved for these cards due to projected future earning potential and the fact that most students already had student loans that were reporting on their credit reports. I had friends that were able to get a Visa or a MasterCard credit card just because they had a student ID. It was too easy! They were giving away credit like Oprah Winfrey! You get a card…you get a card…everybody gets a card! I wanted to take part in this free giveaway also, but I wanted to be a BALLER! I applied for an American Express charge card and was accepted. You see the Visas and the MasterCards had small limits. My American Express didn't' have a limit. I could buy anything I wanted…and I did! I bought clothes, albums, watches, and even rented my first car to take a girl out on a date. This was all within the first month of having the card. I was unstoppable…until that first bill came and I had to slam on the brakes. You see, I did not know the difference between a credit card and a charge card. No one ever told me they were not the same. But I learned the difference very quickly.

I received that first monthly bill and was squirming when I saw that it was over $1,400. But hey, my friends got their bills and only had to send in payments of about $15. My bill didn't have a minimum payment amount on it, so I figured I just had to send in about the same.

That had to be how it worked right? Not so. You see a credit card has a limit that you can utilize, and the payments are based on a formula that will allow you to spread the payments out and make monthly payments on only the amount that you actually use. A charge card is a little different. This type of credit does not limit you on the amount that you can spend. The difference though is that the ENTIRE balance that you use is required to be paid in full each month with the added interest on the amount that you spent. Well, Big Baller Rod did not know that. I sent in a payment to American Express in the amount of…$18.00. I can only imagine the laughter coming from the customer service representative that received my payment. I'm sure they showed my payment to everyone in the office. "Look y'all. This fool spent $1,400 on his card and only sent in a payment of $18.00!" If I allow my imagination eyes to focus, I can see everyone in the office jumping up and down, screaming from pain as their stomach muscles clench from hysteria. But I didn't know any better. I thought I was doing what was expected of me. I found that not to be the case when I received another letter from American Express about a week later returning my $18.00 payment and telling me, per the agreement that I signed when I agreed to accept the charge card, the entire balance spent on the card as well as all applicable interest payments were due in full each month. They included another copy of the bill displaying all of the purchases that I made as well as the balance for the amount owed. I was in trouble. I am now one month past my 18th birthday and I have already begun to mess up my credit. Not because I didn't want to pay my bills, but because I didn't know how credit worked.

As a young man growing up in southern Illinois, I was never actually taught the very important life lesson about the concept of credit or its importance in my life. I used to watch my father from afar as he wrote check after check paying our bills. My mother and father had a mortgage, car loans, and even some credit cards, but never once did we sit down at the table as a family and talk about how they got this credit or its significance in our lives. In the African American family, kids do not get involved in what is considered Grown Folks Business. Due to the struggles of paying bills faced by a lot of families, sometimes it can get dicey, especially when there are more bills than money and parents are deciding between the importance of food over electricity. My parents were able to navigate these decisions and provide a great life for my sister and me. They were able to use credit as a means for survival to supplement their income, but they never told us how they did it. I LOVE MY FAMILY and I appreciate everything that they have ever done for me and continue to do for me. Let me make this point very clear. They did not withhold this information from me purposely! For whatever reason, our culture just does not stress the importance of credit and the advantages you may have by protecting your credit history. That's a very generalized statement I know, but my point is clear – more education for my community is paramount. With that being said, it's now time to go to school.

SO, WHAT IS CREDIT?

So, what exactly IS credit? Credit is obtained when a person or company agrees to provide you a good or a service before payment is received. Both parties to this agreement will negotiate a fee and a term to determine repayment. In other words, credit occurs when someone gives you something and allows you to pay for it later in exchange for a little extra money or interest. Our grandparents used to refer to it as "Paying on Time" or over a period of time. For example, if your car broke down and you needed to get another one, would you have the money to purchase a new car in cash? If the answer is yes, congrats! You are ahead of the curve. If the answer is no, you are among the 90% of Americans that need some form of financing to buy another car. In this example, you would apply for a loan from a bank or finance company in an attempt to purchase the car. The lender would look at your history of repaying other creditors and determine the amount of risk they would endure if they agreed to give you a loan. Utilizing several factors such as your employment stability, income, and previous credit record, the lender would decide whether or not to trust that you would repay the loan if given to you. The better your ability to repay and your prior payment history, the higher the chances of obtaining a loan from a bank or a lender. "Paying on Time!"

There are typically four types of credit offered: 1) Revolving credit, 2) Installment credit, 3) Charge Card credit, and 4) Service credit. With revolving credit, the creditors extend a maximum credit limit and allow you to spend up to that limit. You have the option of paying the balance in full at the end of the month or paying a minimum amount and allowing the balance to carry over into the next month. Most credit cards are revolving credit of some form or another. Installment credit involves a bank or lender giving you a specific amount of money, adding a little interest to the amount, and allowing you to repay in equal monthly installments over a set period of time. Student loans, car loans, and mortgages are examples of installment credit accounts. Charge cards often look like credit cards and are used in a very similar way. Charge cards differ from credit cards in that the credit limits are not set and there is one payment option. The balance of the charge card account is due in full every month…just ask American Express. A term commonly used for charge card accounts is "Net 30" meaning payment is due within 30 days. Service credit is often overlooked and sometimes not even considered credit at all by a lot of people but trust me it is. Service credit is an arrangement between customers and providers of services such as utilities, cell phones, fitness gyms, cable TV, internet and other service-related products that are due and payable each month. Not all service providers report your payment history to the credit bureaus; however, those that do report will definitely inform the credit-reporting agencies when you do not pay on time.

Think of your credit report as a daily journal. This journal is recorded and evaluated by the credit bureaus and details how well or how poorly your financial affairs have been managed. Each day the bureaus record where you live, where you work, and to whom you have associations. Your report is a record of the payment history to each of the creditors that have extended you credit. Although there are several credit-reporting agencies, in the United States the three major companies that most credit providers utilize are Trans Union, Experian, and Equifax. Each of these agencies is a FOR-PROFIT corporation that competes with one another to capture, store, and report credit account payment histories for most US consumers. They receive your payment history on a monthly basis from your creditors and then use this information to create a score based on several factors to evaluate your credit risk and determine whether creditors should extend more credit to you. But what exactly is a credit score, how is it actually calculated, and what can I do with it? Well, I am so glad you asked those questions.

CALCULATING CREDIT SCORES

In 1989, Fair Isaac Corporation introduced a scoring model to lenders that was designed to predict the likelihood of a customer's ability to repay a debt. This closely guarded "secret formula" algorithm was developed to assign a score to consumers based on information obtained from their credit file. The algorithm is so complex that it would not do us any good to try to understand the math even if we knew the actual formula. Although we may not know how to actually calculate your FICO score, we do have a pretty good idea of how it is derived. A FICO score, a derivative of the company's name, ranges from 300 to 850 and groups the information on your credit report into *five* different categories, utilizing a weighted system to calculate your score:

1) **Timeliness of payments** – *35 percent of your score*
   Pay your bills on time to increase your credit scores. One 30-day late payment on a credit card could reduce your score by as many as 110 points. Also, late payments could remain on your report for up to 7 years from the date of the delinquency.

2) **Utilization of credit limits** – *30 percent of your score*
   Credit card utilization is the ratio of the balances of all of your credit cards over the total amount of your credit card limits. Keeping your credit card utilization ratio lower than 30% is best for your credit score. The lower the better!

3) **Length of credit history** – *15 percent of your credit score*

The credit score algorithms calculate your "credit age" by averaging the length of time all of your accounts have been open. The longer your credit accounts have been open and active, the better the influence it has on your credit score.

4) **Mixture of creditors** – *10 percent of your credit score*

To obtain high credit scores, you will need to have a strong mixture of retail accounts, credit cards, installment loans, and mortgages. Repaying all types of debt indicates that you can handle all types of credit.

5) **New credit** – *10 percent of your score*

Applying for and opening new credit should only be done as needed. The impact of credit inquiries varies based on each person's unique credit report.

The term FICO became synonymous with credit scores even though it is not the only scoring model used for credit decisions nor is it without its faults. The FICO score on a specific consumer could be very different depending on the data used by each credit bureau. For example, it is possible to have a FICO score of 680 utilizing information obtained from Trans Union and a FICO score of 600 utilizing information obtained from Equifax for the same consumer. This caused some serious trepidation among lenders when making credit decisions. Since FICO scores were being used during the decision-making process, large differences in scores were allowing some that should not be granted credit to obtain it and some that should be granted credit to suffer. Fair Isaac Corporation unveiled several updates to its model throughout the years, but the three major bureaus still desired a more effective and consistent scoring method.

In 2006, Trans Union, Experian and Equifax teamed up to introduce VantageScore in an effort to make the scoring system more efficient. Similar to the FICO scoring system, VantageScores ranges from 300 to 850. We also do not know the exact formula used to calculate the VantageScore, but we do know how it is derived as well. A

VantageScore groups the information on your report into *six* different categories and utilizes a weighted system to calculate your score:

1) **Timeliness of payments** – *40 percent of your score*

2) **Age and type of credit** – *21 percent of your score*

3) **Utilization of credit limits** – *20 percent of your score*

4) **Account balances** – *11 percent of your score*

5) **Recent credit activities** – *5 percent of your score*
   This category includes recently opened credit accounts as well as recent credit inquiries. These can be indicators of future performance for credit accounts.

6) **Available credit** – *3 percent of your score*
   Even though the effect on your score is small, creditors prefer that you only take out the credit that you need.

According to LendingTree.com, the average FICO score in America is 695 while the average VantageScore is 673. Knowing these credit-affecting factors can help you develop your plan of attack and allow you to build or rebuild your credit history. Now that we know what a credit score is, we must now discover what the score means to creditors. Credit histories usually break down into the following five categories:

- Excellent – 720 credit score or above

- Average – 660-719 credit score

- Fair – 620-659 credit score

- Poor – 580-619 credit score

- Very Poor – 579 or below

These numbers are very subjective and vary from company to company but are generally the ranges used when determining creditworthiness. A no credit score results when you do not have accounts reporting on your credit report and a score cannot be calculated. Although I do not believe that a score alone can fully define a person and their actual intent to repay, each year over 25 BILLION credit decisions are made based *solely* on these credit scores. That being said, your credit history does provide a glimpse of your character, your reliability, and your trustworthiness.

Having an excellent credit rating can impact several different areas in your life. Credit ratings influence whether a bank or finance company will give you a loan for a house, a car, or a business. Credit ratings can decide the rate at which you will pay back these loans. The lower the credit rating, the higher the interest rate IF the creditors even decide to approve your request. But credit ratings also play a part in areas of our life that we don't usually think about such as insurance rates, employment, and bank accounts. Begin to make it a habit to check your credit score at least once a week (but more on that later). We must learn to protect our credit rating just as we protect our children. Each individual has a unique credit file linked to them by their social security number. Because of this, it is almost impossible to get a new credit file. There are a few very extreme cases for which the government may issue a new social security number, but for the most part, your number is your number. If you have been faced with previous credit issues, you can't petition the Social Security Administration to give you a new number just because you messed up your credit in the past. You did the proverbial crime, now you must do the proverbial time. You were a prisoner to debt. Now you must go through the process of rehabilitating your finances and getting your financial second chance.

If you are like many of us (yes, I said us), you may have done some stupid stuff in your past that resulted in negative items being placed on your credit report (Thank you again, American Express). To this point, you have lived with the reality that there are some things you will not be able to do or have as a result of past credit indiscretions. Now we can take the Donald Trump approach and file for bankruptcy protection, but unless you have millions of dollars hidden in a secret vault or a wealthy friend or family member to sponsor you, that will take up to ten years to correct. <u>Bankruptcy is a last resort, not a first level of defense.</u> Filing for bankruptcy protection for the average person is like having a Scarlet "B" placed on their credit history for at least ten years. Although bankruptcy in certain situations can be very necessary, consider the aftereffects before delving into that direction. The road to redemption can be daunting, but with patience, planning, and persistence you can maneuver through the stages of recovery and achieve the financial freedom you desire.

So I start my mission – leave my residence
Thinking how can I get some dead presidents...

Eric B. & Rakim

CHAPTER 1 HOT TAKES

1. Commit yourself to developing your Master Plan.

2. Admit to yourself that you have financial problems. You will not be able to *fix* the problem until you *admit* the problem.

3. Mistakes are human nature. No one is perfect. Use your past mistakes as a learning tool.

4. Credit in itself is not good, however, in today's society it is a necessity. Do not forget the designed purpose of credit.

5. Understand the types of credit offered and only utilize the credit that you need.

6. Learn how credit scores are calculated and the weighted percentages for each category. Always check your credit report.

7. Know the difference between a good credit score and a bad credit score.

8. Begin to make it a habit to check your credit score at least once a week.

THE
PROCESS

—

CHAPTER TWO

CHAPTER 2 – THE PROCESS

At the end of the 2012-2013 NBA season, the Philadelphia 76ers found themselves in a very precarious position. After having lost in the first round of the playoffs the previous two years to much better teams in the Miami Heat and Boston Celtics, the Sixers finished the 2012-13 season with a record of 34 wins and 48 losses and missed the playoffs entirely. The Sixers had a problem. They were faced with a rapidly growing payroll, an aging and underperforming roster, and roadblocks in the form of Kevin Garnett, Paul Pierce, Dwayne Wade, and Lebron James to name a few. They could not see the pot at the end of the rainbow, so the decision was made to rebuild their team by developing a plan that would later become known as "The Process." In the star-driven league that is the NBA, several **superstars** are needed to compete for championships in today's game. The Sixers did not have any superstars, so changes were necessary. They believed that the only way to compete against the Heat and the Celtics would be to amass multiple high draft picks and build their team with young, cost-effective lottery picks. Whether or not this was a good strategy is debatable, but nevertheless it came with a great caveat. In order to obtain these high draft picks, the team had to lose…and lose…and lose…and lose. From 2013 through 2017, the team lost 253 games while winning only 75, never once making the playoffs. This much losing caused even the most diehard fans to want to give up on their team. The more the Sixers worked their "Process," the more the fans bemoaned and became disenchanted, arguing and bickering over the direction the team was headed. It was very hard watching as the Sixers continued to lose games, but they stayed the course. They had a plan that they believed would lead them towards an NBA Championship and continued to "Work the Process." They believed in the Process and implemented their plan. Today they have two of the best young players in the league, money available on their salary cap to attract star free agents, and several future draft picks to continue to build their team around. They have begun to win games and "The Process" has now worked in Philadelphia. An adaptation of Ecclesiastes 9:11 states, "The race is not given to the swift nor the battle to the strong, but he who endures until the end." In order to erase a lifetime of bad habits, you must develop your own "process" and implement your plan to the end. The process of cleaning your credit is actually pretty similar to the Sixers situation. You may have lost…and lost…and lost…and lost with your bad credit decisions. Losing in the credit game can cause even the strongest person to want to give up on trying to fix their credit situation or become disenchanted. Like the Sixers, stay the course. Believe in the Process. Work the plan.

> proc·ess / ˈprä͟ses,ˈprō͟ses/
> *noun*
> 1. **A series of actions or steps taken in order to achieve a particular end.**[13]

PROCESS IMPLEMENTATION

The first series of actions needed in implementing our plan includes establishing an excellent credit score. Remember that an excellent credit score is one that is greater than a 720 FICO. The plan is to create a credit score such that most loan requests will be approved, and you are able to receive the lowest interest rates and payments possible. This will be achieved by correcting any errors or misinformation that is showing on your report, diversifying the types of credit you have contained on your report, and eliminating as much of your debt as possible while retaining your credit limits. According to the Federal Trade Commission (FTC), over 75 percent of all credit reports contain errors of some sort, with 20 percent of all reports containing "potentially material errors."[6] An error can be as small as an incorrect balance reporting on an account to as large as having an account that does not belong to you reporting. Whatever the type of inaccuracy, any error could possibly cause your credit score to suffer. When one point could be the difference between a 1.9% interest rate and an 8.9% interest rate on an auto loan, every point counts!

Begin your plan by obtaining a copy of your credit report from each of the three major credit-reporting agencies. Subscribing to one of several credit monitoring services will allow you to see your credit score on a daily basis. Credit reports pulled by you without the desire to request credit are considered soft credit pulls, while credit reports pulled by others in an attempt to verify information or extend credit are considered hard credit pulls. Soft credit pulls do not affect your credit score, whereas hard credit pulls could possibly reduce your credit score. A free credit monitoring service such as Credit Karma will allow you to view your credit file constantly without affecting your credit score. This site will allow you to see your Trans Union (TU) and Equifax (EQ) reports as well as giving you a credit score for reference purposes only.

Other sites such as Credit Check Total work just as well but will require a subscription to view the reports. With Credit Check Total, you will be able to view your Experian (EX) report as well as your Trans Union and Equifax. Whatever your choice for credit monitoring services, obtain a report from all three bureaus to begin the process.

Purchase a 3-ring binder and place a copy of each report into your new "credit binder," separating and labeling each credit-reporting agency with dividers. If using a tri-merged credit report, place a copy of the report in each section of your binder and highlight each account that is reporting on the corresponding bureau. In this stage of the Credit Process, you are trying to correct any account or personal information that could possibly have a negative effect on your credit score. Review all of the personal information listed on the reports. Make sure you do not have multiple names or addresses listed on the report. Variations of your name or old addresses can cause errors to report on your credit history. Multiple addresses show instability or someone that jumps around and may cause a reduction in your score. If your work history is showing, verify that it is current and accurate. Multiple jobs reporting presents a picture of instability and could also have a negative effect on your credit score. Review all hard inquiries, credit accounts, collections, and public records and take note of anything that is deemed inaccurate or negative. Make a list of all erroneous information that is currently showing on your report, no matter how huge or miniscule. Also list all accounts that have negative histories, missed payments, incorrect balances, or anything that needs correction or deletion. Record the name of the creditor, the contact information, the account number, and any other information that you deem important such as opening date, closing date, and reporting date. This information will be necessary for the next steps in improving your credit rating. Now that you know what is on your report and what needs to be off of it, let's talk strategy to improve your score and lead you further down the road to financial freedom *(Sample credit report in Appendix A).*

CLEAN UP WHAT YOU MESSED UP

You were the man in college,
Got a degree in awesome
And had more zeroes in your bank than all the Matrix
    coding
Now you're in your mama's basement
'Cause you spend every paycheck
The IRS your new best friend
That's how you know you messed up
    That's How You Know by Nico & Vinz

Do you know how you messed up? Then good. Let's fix what you messed up! Nico & Vinz used another word for "messed" that's considered a little harsher, but I will keep it clean. But if you are anything like I was, the original word is probably more applicable. Don't fret...there is hope! There are several different strategies available to you when you are trying to improve your credit score. I think I may have tried twenty of them (heck, it was probably fifty of them) before I found a method that actually worked for me. Okay I may be exaggerating on the number a tad bit, but it was DEFINITELY a lot!!! If you look between the lines you will see my point: DON'T GIVE UP TRYING. According to the federal Fair Credit Reporting Act (FCRA), you have the right to challenge any incomplete or inaccurate information that may be reporting on your credit history. What this means is that ANYTHING incorrect, in any form or fashion, can be challenged. Think of an NFL football game and you are the coach. You are given a red flag that can be thrown to challenge a call on the field if you feel that the referees missed a call or made a wrong interpretation of the rule. The league office then looks at the play in question, verifies whether the play was officiated correctly, and then returns a conclusion on its accuracy.

Same principle. If you identify incorrect information on your report, throw the red flag and challenge it. The credit-reporting agencies must then take a closer look at your information, verify whether it is reporting correctly with your creditors, and return with a conclusion on its legitimacy and accuracy. According to the FCRA, a creditor has up to 30 days to verify that the account information they are reporting to the credit bureaus is accurate. If the creditor does not respond within the 30 days or if any discrepancies are found with the reporting of the account information, the law states that the item must be removed immediately. Inaccurate, incomplete or unverifiable information must be removed or corrected, however, if the information is found to be correct, the creditors can continue to report the account history as before. This law has given the consumer a tool that could be utilized to help correct some prior credit indiscretions. It has been utilized by thousands of credit repair companies in the past who have written dispute letters on behalf of their customers. They have been able to remove millions of inaccurate accounts from credit reports that allow their customers to increase their credit scores and obtain the additional credit they desire. Hiring a credit repair company has worked extremely well in the past, but lately they have been met with some serious opposition.

Because of the high volume of dispute letters received from third party companies, the credit reporting agencies began classifying some letters received from these credit repair agencies as frivolous and are not investigating the authenticity of their claims. This is a process that the credit-reporting agencies refer to as "jamming," a practice whereby the credit repair agencies would send multiple dispute letters for the same account with the hopes that it would "fall through the cracks" and jam up the credit dispute procedure. Joanne S. Faulkner, a Connecticut consumer protection attorney argued, "The volume and spurious nature of the disputes sent by credit repair organizations intentionally interferes with the credit bureaus' business of providing accurate reports."[14] She also stated "The credit repair organizations' systematic deception of the credit bureaus and of consumers undermines the banking system and harms consumers and creditors alike."[14] As a result of jamming, the credit bureaus began sending letters to the consumers informing them of their rights according to the FCRA and announcing that some third party claims will no longer be investigated due to this procedure.

CHAPTER 2 – THE PROCESS

Now I cannot guarantee that everything in this book will work for you. Nothing is 100% in the arena of credit repair. But what I will try to give you are strategies to help with your process. The credit repair industry itself can be very "scammish." I know that is not a word, but my point is there are many credit repair companies that will tell you that all you need to do is send a dispute letter to the credit bureaus and your score will increase from under 500 to over 740 in 30 days. While definitely a possible outcome, that is not very probable. There is a very important point to remember when trying to repair your credit. If it didn't take you 30 days to ruin your credit, how can it take you 30 days to repair it? Be very weary of a company that tells you this will all be done in a month. Be even "more weary" of a company that tells you to pay them large sums of money up front before they have done any work for you. No matter how successful a company has been in the past, they cannot guarantee that your credit will be cleared of past indiscretions. Every attempt at credit repair is different just like a snowflake; therefore, it requires a new strategy each time it is attempted. In other words, what works for Raquel may not work for Rodney.

Although the waters may get murky when dealing with a credit repair company, they are not all bad and are very useful and competent when attempting to fix your credit situation. If you are not very comfortable attempting your own credit repair, use the Internet to research credit repair companies. Find a company that has good customer reviews and a proven success rate in your attempt to correct discrepancies on your report. Just know that the services provided by these companies can be attempted by you for free. If you do a search for a credit dispute letter, you will find hundreds of sites that will have samples. Using one of these samples as a guide, you can create your own letters to send to the credit bureaus to dispute inaccuracies on your report. At the end of the day, the goal is to clear your credit history of any negative items. It really doesn't matter which method is used, as long as you get the desired end result *(Sample dispute letter in Appendix B)*.

Any inaccurate information on your credit report may have an adverse effect on your credit score. That is why it is very important to make sure all of your personal information is correct. Correcting personal information can be achieved either by letter, online, or via telephone. We will begin with the telephone option because it is the easiest and fastest option to correct personal information *(Bureau phone numbers in Appendix C)*. Call each number and let them know that you would like to dispute the incorrect personal information that is reporting on your credit history. Verify your correct information with the bureau's customer service representative and request that the erroneous information be removed immediately. Now in a perfect world, this should work fine. Unfortunately you are not in a perfect world. Your call may get connected to a representative that is having a very bad day and does not want to help you. They may tell you that you will need to submit a written request along with supporting documentation in order to dispute this information. At this point, quickly hang up the phone, call the number again, and talk with another representative. The Hang Up, Call Back method will eventually work, just keep trying as much as necessary.

If you can't get any help from the credit company representatives or get tired of this method, move on to the written dispute process. Send each of the credit bureaus a letter of dispute requesting that all incorrect personal information be removed from your credit report. Include a list of any addresses, alias, employment, and telephone numbers that are not current. The online dispute process will require that you sign up for the credit monitoring services offered by each bureau. This will require a financial commitment on your part, but it works well also. Sign into your created account and select the dispute option on all of the information that you want removed. The bureaus will immediately start the investigation process based on the reason that you selected for each account. Correcting personal information is the easiest part of the repair process. This step builds up your confidence and encourages you to move on to the more intense steps.

TIME TO GET DOWN TO THE NITTY GRITTY!!!

In the 1984 song "Five Minutes of Funk," Whodini said the phrase, "But now we're gettin' down to the nitty gritty." For us, the nitty gritty we are talking about is the hard process of credit cleaning. Now that you have gotten your personal information corrected, a harder step in our Master Plan is attempting to remove hard credit inquiries from your report. There are two ways of pulling your credit report; a soft credit inquiry and a hard credit inquiry. A soft credit inquiry occurs when your credit file is accessed for things such as a credit preapproval, an employer inquiry, or a credit website such as Credit Karma where credit decisions are not being made. Most of the time these types of credit pulls are done without your knowledge and do not affect your credit score. A hard credit inquiry occurs when you actually apply for credit such as a credit card, a car loan, or a mortgage. Hard inquiries could slightly reduce your credit score and will stay on your credit history for two years. Although the weighted percentage for credit inquiries is relatively low, every point counts when you are trying to increase your credit score. You will want to dispute any hard credit inquiry from a creditor that did not extend you credit. For example, if you were attempting to purchase a car and the dealer sent your loan application to 8 different lenders before finding one that gave you the best terms, you want to dispute the other 7 to have those inquiries removed. You can't dispute the company that actually provided you the loan. Yes, I know about how the credit bureaus only count multiple credit pulls as one when attempting to purchase a car or obtain a mortgage. You want them removed anyway. Numerous inquiries on your history look like you were unable to obtain credit from other lenders or that you were desperate for credit, which is just as bad. This could make other prospective lenders question your ability to repay and deny your loan or give you very unfavorable terms if they decide to approve your application at all. As with correcting your personal information, a letter, phone call, or online dispute will work towards removing these inquiries. From experience, attempt to call the bureaus first and if unsuccessful, follow that up with a letter of dispute such as the one found in the Appendix. This will be your first test. Removing inquiries can tend to be a little difficult. A lot of people will give up on this step considering the limited number of points gained from fewer inquiries. DON'T FALL INTO THAT TRAP! Keep at it. Stay the course. If the bureaus deny your request, send another letter…and another. Trust me when I say it will pay off in the end.

So you put a checkmark next to the task of tackling credit inquiries. Now you must attempt to tackle the even more difficult task of eliminating the negatives. This is where the fun begins…the *Grittiest of the Nitty*!!! The goal in your pathway to credit restoration is eliminating all negative items that may show up on your credit report, whether correct or incorrect. Since timeliness of payments represents 35% of your credit score, I am sure you will agree that this task is very important. You can accomplish this task with a series of dispute letters sent to the credit bureaus and/or the collection agencies or online utilizing the dispute options on the credit bureau sites. (Quick note: if utilizing the online option and the information comes back verified, you will not be able to dispute that account again using the same reason.) By law you have the right to request that any collection agency validate an alleged debt. Validation is different from verification in that the collection agency must produce proof that you actually signed the alleged debt and that they have legal standing to attempt to collect on the debt.

Request in writing that the collection agency provide proof of your signature on the original contract, a payment history, copy of the agreement with the client that authorizes the collection agency to collect on the allege account, and other pertinent documents regarding the alleged debt. Inform the collection agency that they have 30 days to return the requested information or you will be forced to take additional measures. Send the debt validation letter to each collection agency via certified mail requiring a signature. This will give you a paper trail of all correspondence. Place a copy of the letter and the mailing receipt into your folder for your records *(Sample Debt Validation letter in Appendix*

D). If after receiving the requested information from the collection agency it is determined that the information is incorrect or erroneous, we will proceed to send what we like to call a 609 letter. According to Section 609 of the Fair Credit Reporting Act (FCRA), the burden of proof is placed on the collection agencies and the credit bureaus to provide proof an account is legitimately yours. It is the Consumers Disclosure section that provides for the protection of consumers against false and erroneous reporting. The FCRA was enacted by Congress to protect consumers from unverifiable accounts and inaccurate information being stated on their credit report. It is the responsibility of the credit bureaus to verify AND validate **_every single entry_** that appears on your credit report. We will make them do their job!

If the collection agencies actually provide the information that you requested, don't worry. All is not lost. Another way of clearing negative items off of your report is to pay any past debt that may be negatively affecting your score. This sounds simple if you actually have the money available, but it actually requires a lot of negotiation skills. If you only pay off your debt without negotiating the proper terms, the account will begin to show as 'paid', but not 'paid as agreed'. It will continue to remain on your history and could still negatively affect your credit score even when paid because the prior negative remarks remained. Remember negative items can still affect your score even when paid for up to 7 years. Your defined goal is to improve your credit history. You want to accomplish this by having any negative accounts *permanently* erased from your history. This will be done by never accepting "NO" for an answer. Your goal right now is "Pay-for-Deletion." At this point, you can either call the collection agency and speak with a customer service representative concerning paying off the account in exchange for a letter of deletion or send a certified letter to the collection agency offering to pay the debt in exchange for a letter of deletion.

Depending on the age of the debt, you may also be able to negotiate a settlement that is lower than the original amount owed. If the opportunity arises, of course you would like to spend the least amount of money possible, however, this is not your main goal. The amount of your settlement is your personal choice. Remember that some collection agencies purchase your debts for pennies on the dollar and are in the business of making money. For example, if you owed $1,000 on the original debt and the collection agency purchased the debt for 15%, they actually paid $150 for your debt. Let's assume your offer for Pay-to-Deletion was $500. That would be a good business deal for the "for-profit" collection agency. Always present your offer as a business deal and try to make sure the offer makes good business sense for all parties involved. The position of the creditor is to receive payment on the outstanding account in question. Initially they may not accept your business proposition, but do not take "NO" for an answer. Continue going up the chain of command until you reach the person authorized to agree to your terms. If necessary, use the story of your life and the reason you are trying to clear up your credit history as a way to convince the customer service representative to accept your request of removing the account. For example, if you had a job layoff that caused your credit to suffer, use that fact. This is a sample conversation you may have with your creditor:

> *"Madame Creditor, I understand that I did not live up to the terms of our agreement, but I had some very extenuating circumstances that caused some serious personal hardships. I have been attempting to correct my previous issues by living up to the agreements that I signed. I am trying my best to make things better for my family*

after such a difficult period and I am hoping that I may find some favor in the sights of your company.

Right now I am able to attempt to rectify this problem so that I will not be forced to seek bankruptcy protection on this account. I have come up with the $1,000 that I currently owe your company, but I am faced with a serious dilemma. I can use the money to pay my debt with you thereby satisfying our agreement, but that will not fix my credit issue because the account will still report as negative. Or I can use this money to file for bankruptcy protection to eliminate all of my outstanding debt and start over.

I would much prefer to pay my debt, but just paying you will not help me with my credit recovery. I am willing to send you the full payment immediately if you would be willing to send me a letter stating that the account will be removed from my credit history completely. I realize that this is not a common request, but it will allow me to fulfill my obligation to you as well as avoid another account being placed on a bankruptcy filing.

My attorney has advised against this request, but I am hoping that we may be able to come to an agreement so that I do not have to include this account in any bankruptcy filings. Is this something that you can help me with or do I need to speak with someone else regarding this matter?"

If you have read this and wondered why my tone has changed, well there is a method to my madness. Never once have I seen anyone get anything done to their benefit by not speaking in a kind and businesslike manner. I was always taught to kill someone with kindness. No matter the response you get from the associate, continue killing them with kindness. Even if they do not give you the answers you seek, kill them with more kindness. The fact remains that the person on the other end of the phone is a human just like you and is probably facing the same types of situations that you are calling about. By you talking in this business-like tone, you will be able to attract more with your honey than your vinegar.

During the negotiation of the debt, inform the creditor that you are willing to send payment IMMEDIATELY if they would agree to send you a signed letter stating that the account will be removed once paid. This is actually a simple request for the creditor. Their primary goal is to get the debt paid. They are not the credit bureaus, so it really does not benefit them to deny taking your money. The problem is precedence. They do not want the precedence to be set and known that they are willing to erase bad items in lieu of money. Creditors, as a coalition, want to make sure that other creditors know about the payment histories of prospective applicants. If they all erased delinquent payments just because they received what is owed, the credit bureaus would be useless. But the fact of the matter is they do this all of the time. That is why you need to appeal to the human side of "Madame Creditor."

For creditors, the most important thing for them is receiving payment. They really do not care about your personal credit rating, only their fiscal bottom line. As the saying goes, "If it makes money, then it makes sense." If the creditors are getting the money that is owed to them, they will, for the most part, agree to your offer. If "Madame Creditor" says no, either call back and speak with another agent or ask to speak with someone higher in the chain of command that may be able to accept your offer as suggested. You must keep calling and talking to people until they accept your offer. Eventually they will. At the end of the day, the only thing the creditor wants is their money. The same process can be achieved with a Pay-for-Deletion letter sent to the collection agency via certified mail *(Sample Pay-for-Deletion letter in Appendix E)*. One thing to remember during this portion of the process is to not make ANY payments on the accounts until you receive a signed acceptance of your proposition. Once accepted, send the payment via Money Order, Cashier's Check, or pre-paid credit card. Never give banking information or personal debit card numbers. You do not want to run the risk of any "mistakes" being made when processing the payments by the collection agency. Place a copy of the form of payment in your Trapper. From here, *"Lather, Rinse, Repeat."* Once you have assembled all of your letters from your creditors and collection agencies, forward these letters to each of the three credit bureaus. You must forward to each bureau separately because they are competing companies and do not share information between businesses. Once received, they will immediately remove the negative items from your credit history possibly increasing your credit score. The amount of the increase will depend on the positive items remaining on your credit history. In order to become financially free, you must have an excellent credit rating. That may sound like an oxymoron – you need excellent credit to become financially free. As you continue to work your plan, this fact will come into focus a little more. Your plan is beginning to take form, but keep being dedicated to improving your credit rating and don't stop there. Maintain your newly found excellent credit rating as you continue to work your plan. This first step of improving your credit rating is extremely important as you continue to build towards financial freedom.

> *You wanna know what's more important*
> *than throwin' away money at a strip club?*
> *Credit!*

The Story of O.J. by Jay-Z

CHAPTER 2 HOT TAKES

1. Sign up with a Credit Monitoring service to always have an eye on your credit history.

2. Make sure your credit report is 100% accurate.

3. Try disputing any incorrect information with the credit bureaus to correct any irregularities on your report.

4. Remember the fact that it did not take you 30 days to mess up your credit. How can it take 30 days to fix it? THIS IS A PROCESS.

5. Use the Fair Credit Reporting Act (FCRA) as a tool to help fix errors on your credit report.

6. When trying to negotiate with creditors, DO NOT TAKE "NO" FOR AN ANSWER...and don't give up!!!

7. In some instances, Pay For Deletion is an excellent way to correct an account.

DREAM
TO GET
C.R.E.A.M.

—

CHAPTER THREE

CHAPTER 3 – DREAM TO GET C.R.E.A.M.

nother reminder of the ubiquitous foothold Hip-Hop has ingrained into our culture came in 1993 with the first publication of Vibe Magazine. Founded and launched by the musical legend Quincy Jones, Vibe Magazine provided insight into the world of entertainment and music with a focus on Hip-Hop and R&B artists. As a Hip-Hop fan, 1993 was one of the best years ever! Tupac gave us "Holla If You Hear Me," MC-Lyte needed a "Ruffneck," Cypress Hill was "Insane in the Membrane," and Digital Underground taught us the "Humpty Dance." It was a great time to be a fan of the Hip-Hop culture. Then came November 9, 1993 when the world of Hip-Hop "was about to Blow Up!!!" (in my Martin Lawrence voice) On this one day in music history, we were blessed to have received what could only be considered two totally complete musical masterpieces: Wu Tang Clan's debut release, **Enter the Wu Tang (36 Chambers)**, and A Tribe Called Quest third album, **Midnight Marauders**. Both albums were wonderful from beginning to end, but that was about all they would have in common. These albums could not be more different with Tribe and its smooth jazz feel and Wu with its raw, thugged-out grit. Both are widely regarded as two of the most influential Hip-Hop albums of the 90's and amongst the greatest Hip-Hop albums ever. I thought I was HARD in 1993 so I gravitated towards **Enter the Wu Tang**. I remember driving in my car with the cassette blasting as we got ourselves ready to run somebody's basketball court. We would just put in the tape to get pumped and ready to dominate with our hoop game. *Bring da Ruckus*, *Method Man*, *Protect Ya Neck*, and of course *C.R.E.A.M. – these were the jams*! (For my younger readers, a jam is a song that you like a lot ☺) I can still remember bobbing my head to C.R.E.A.M. in my steel blue Pontiac Firebird: "A man with a dream with plans to make cream." The hook was catchy and made you want to yell out: *"Cash rules everything around me, C.R.E.A.M get the money, Dollar, Dollar Bill Y'all."* Because of this song, CREAM became synonymous with money in our daily dialogue. It was everyone's mission to get the CREAM. Even today those words still ring true – cash truly does rule everything around us. You need cash for food, clothing, housing – CREAM, education, transportation, and anything else you could imagine – CREAM! Your financial freedom revolves around you and your CREAM. Because of this circle of CREAM, you need to develop more ways of getting your money and even more ways of stacking it. We need to stack our cash so that our future family tree will not need to struggle for the basic necessities of life. We need to stack our cash so that we can enjoy things in this life, prepare our family for the future life, and not have to stress about how we are going to pay our bills. We just discussed "The Master Plan," now we need to discuss your "Dream to get C.R.E.A.M."

> *It's been (fifty) long hard years, I'm still strugglin'*
> *Survival got me buggin', but I'm alive on arrival*
> *I peep at the shape of the streets*
> *And stay awake to the ways of the world cause (stuff) is deep.*
> **C.R.E.A.M. by Wu Tang Clan**

BEFORE THE FALL

I used to work as a mortgage broker where I helped people realize their dreams of owning a home. That was a very rewarding job, both emotionally and financially. At the same time, I was able to help myself with a good income and help others by fulfilling their dreams of home ownership. The income generated from originating mortgages was ENORMOUS and the process was quick and easy!!! All you needed was a customer that had the desire to own a home, a job, and a little money, and you could get them approved and closed on their new mortgage in no time. The guidelines were so lax that I was literally able to take an application in the morning and have the loan closed and funded by that evening. Charles Dickens described it best in *A Tale of Two Cities* when he said, "It was the best of times, it was the worst of times. It was the season of light, it was the season of darkness. It was the spring of hope, it was the winter of sadness,"[15] because then 2007 hit.

In July of 2007, I received a fax from Countrywide Home Loans, the number one company for mortgage originations, stating that they would be closed for a few hours and would not be accepting any additional applications until the afternoon. I remember this because it struck me as kind of odd at the time. I began to receive phone calls from representatives from other lenders asking me if I had heard any of the rumors of Countrywide closing down. I could not believe the noise because Countrywide was one of the biggest lenders around. Sure, others had closed previously, but they were the smaller lenders that did not have the buying power of a company like Countrywide. Surely these rumors had to be false because there was no way a large lender could close down. Well, about three hours later we received another fax stating that Countrywide was not closing but would no longer be accepting loan origination packages. Ouch did that hurt because I had several loans in underwriting at the time. What I was going to do about my loans was really the only thing I was concerned about at the time. Then as they say the proverbial "stuff" started to hit the fan. Over the next few months, lender after lender started sending faxes saying that they were suspending the underwriting of all files until further notice. Before long, we were involved in the worse financial crisis since the Great Depression of the 1930's. Today with the way that our economy is going, "stuff" IS getting deep. You need to stay awake and become more aware of what's going on in your own financial world. In order for you to get the CREAM, you must develop a plan of action to curtail your spending and to begin saving. In other words, you need a budget.

B.U.D.G.E.T.

Sometimes we think of the word BUDGET as a bad word – a curse word. We feel that if we enact a budget on our lives, we will not be able to do the things that we like to do or buy the things that we like to buy. That is not necessarily true. Sure, a budget will put some constraints on our spending, but it does not mean we always have to sacrifice. The purpose of a budget is to create a plan that guarantees you have enough money to spend on the things that you need and the things that you want. Budgeting helps to keep you from incurring any unnecessary debt as well as assisting with reducing your current debt. A budget is very necessary and very crucial to your financial health. There is a very important reason why you want to develop a budget:

<u>B</u>ecause
<u>U</u>
<u>D</u>on't
<u>G</u>et
<u>E</u>verything
<u>T</u>aken

Yes, I know that I took license on the U, but you understand the point. The purpose of having a budget is to make sure that you have enough money to cover your expenses and begin to prepare for a life of freedom. You want a budget to prevent overspending and running the risk of having your assets taken, if you can't afford to pay for them. Budgets also allow you to further protect the great credit score that you so painstakingly developed. The most commonly accepted rule of budgeting is to spend _at most_ 70 percent of your monthly income on expenses and utilize _at least_ 30 percent of your income for investments and savings. If you were to consider your current income and expenses, would you fall within this 70/30 rule?

In its simplest form, a budget is easy to understand. The problem again goes back to dedication and commitment. If you are not dedicated and committed to your budget, you are wasting your time and wasting your money. You might as well continue to live day-to-day and week-to-week; keep surviving and not living. When you begin to live, you will develop your budget and implement all of its aspects, working harder and harder everyday to make sure you attain your goals. If you are just surviving, you probably do not have a plan and are not adhering to the 70/30 rule. You are probably not even adhering to a 90/10 rule for that matter! How do you alleviate this problem? How do you hit the reset button? You do this by planning and using technology.

With the tools available to us at the touch of a button, you can develop your budget, keep track of your spending, and create more financial flexibility. Consider and research different financial planning software. These programs are a very good way of developing your budget and keeping track of your spending every second of the day. You can enter all of your expenses and the programs will keep a categorized listing of how you are spending your money. This is important because with the categorized data, you can calculate how you are currently spending and how you should be actually be spending. How many days a week do you eat out at a restaurant? How many specialty coffees do you purchase? How many Pepsis? How many adult beverages do you buy? These are just a few of the things you will begin to realize are preventing you from having more financial freedom. The bottom line for most families is that you may earn enough money to live, but you generally spend it all on your homes, your cars, your credit cards, and your other perceived necessities. You usually leave very little for saving or investing. You are not protected when an unexpected emergency hits home. If you lose a job or get sick, you are not financially equipped to handle the aftermath. When you hear politicians say that the middle class is eroding, that is because a large portion of the working middle class has become "fragile" for lack of planning and lack of savings. The only way that we can reverse this trend is to begin to live within our means, to reduce our expenditures, and to search for other sources of income to prevent our own personal recession.   With the financial software, you will be able to log all of your spending on your computers or mobile devices, have access to your all of your spending, and know exactly where your money is going at all times. I am sure you have heard of the popular proverb, **"Knowledge is power."** It simply means that knowledge is more powerful than physical strength and no great work can be done without knowledge. Knowledge is a formidable factor that empowers people to achieve great results. The more knowledge a person gains, the more powerful they become. Now that you have this newfound knowledge, let's begin to see how powerful it can be for your budget!

Did you know that eighty-five percent of all Americans believe that no matter how much or how little money they make, they will be able to live on that amount? Or that one in three Americans will save $0 for retirement? Or worse yet, fifty-five percent of all Americans spend up to their income or beyond their income EACH MONTH…in other words "Living Paycheck to Paycheck"? That's not good. That's not good at all. You must find a way to save money for retirement, for pleasure, and for emergencies. You can't rely on Social Security or other programs to sustain you in your golden years. Who REALLY wants to be the greeter at Wal-Mart? I know I don't! It is never too late to start saving, but the time to develop your plan and your budget is now! According to statistics released by the US Department of Labor, the median income in the United States equaled $69,629 in 2015.[16] This calculates to be about $5,800 per month in gross income with about $4,250 per month in net income. One of the most important things to remember when developing your budget is to base all of the numbers on your net income or take-home pay because as they say in Las Vegas, Uncle Sam takes his "vig" off of the top. Using the "70/30" rule, $2,975 should be allocated for all of your expenses consisting of both fixed costs and variable costs. Think of it this way, fixed cost are things that you must pay for each month that you "have no choice but to pay" – things such as mortgage/rent, car payments, student loans, insurance, groceries, and utilities. Variable costs include things such as credit cards, gas, specialty coffees, take-out restaurants, clothes, movies, and adult beverages that you "choose to pay."

Using Appendix F, list your take-home income, fixed expenses, and variable expenses. Now subtract the expenses from your take-home income. Is that number positive or negative? If the number is negative, then you REALLY must start developing your budget NOW! If the number is positive, then you are living within the amount that you are making. That is a good thing! But how positive is the number? Do you have $200 left over? How about $450? Well using our rule of "70/30," you should have $1,275 left over for saving and investing. If you are not at that number or if your number is negative, you need to do one of two things: cut your expenses (which we will tackle now) or make more money (which we will tackle later). When you sit down to begin your own budget, consider all of your incoming funds and your outgoing expenses. Use Appendix F as a guideline for your budgeting plan.

WHERE YOUR C.R.E.A.M. GOES

According to the site NerdWallet.com, the average US household has about $131,000 of debt including credit cards, auto loans, mortgages, student loans and other financial obligations.[17] Below you will find a typical list of monthly expenses for the average American household:

CURRENT BUDGETED EXPENSES	
MORTGAGE/RENT	$1,060.00
CAR NOTE	$469.00
INSURANCES (LIFE, HEALTH, AUTO, HOME)	$514.00
CREDIT CARDS (MINIMUMS)	$189.00
UTILITIES (GAS, WATER, ELECTRIC)	$225.00
COMMUNICATION (INTERNET & CELL)	$265.00
STUDENT LOANS	$280.00
FOOD	$550.00
ENTERTAINMENT	$300.00
GAS	$368.00
TOTAL	**$4,220.00**

As you can see, this is a survival budget. The typical American has only $30 left over each month for savings. That equates to a whopping $360 at the end of the year. Now tell me, what kind of vacation can you have with $360? Maybe a one-night stay at a hotel with dinner and a movie. How does that sound? I don't know about you, but that is just not working for me! If I work hard all year, I want a little bit of a vacation at least. It doesn't have to be Paris or London, but it sure can be San Diego, and $360 just ain't cutting it, no matter the destination. So what do you do? You fall right back into the trap of spending even more on your credit cards and continuing to fall further and further into debt. But here is the problem – for most of us this is the rule and not the exception. The most common misconception is that if someone does not have a lot of savings, they are wasting money. As you can plainly see from the previous example, the average American family is not wasting a lot of money. Most of their expenses are for things that they perceive to be important and necessary. There is always room for improvement. Now take a look at *your* budget sheet. How much is your net monthly income? How much are your monthly expenses? What are your fixed and variable expenses? With this information we can begin to develop your optimal spending plan and prevent your budget from being for lack of a better phrase, "out of whack!"

TARGETED C.R.E.A.M.

One of the requirements to graduate from high school was passing an economics class where you began to learn the basic skills needed to develop a budget. You learned how to write checks, balance your checkbook, and pay bills. You learned these skills at the time because you were forced. You were still too young to realize that bills would soon control your future and budgeting would mean the difference between prosperity and bankruptcy. I am living proof of the perils of not developing a budget, and now I am here to "kick some truth" to all of my people about its importance. If I were to think about all of the money that I wasted in my lifetime, that number would be astounding. I could only imagine where I would have been financially had I invested that wasted money. How much better could my life have been? Or my family's life? Well, the truth of the matter is that I didn't...so now what? Let me tell you what now?! I have dedicated myself to eliminating debt and sacrificing things for the greater good...living!

A lifetime of spending without a long-term goal of savings has brought you to this point in time. You have grown accustomed to living your current lifestyle and any changes to that lifestyle, in a negative way, will not be received well by you or your entire family. You will need to make some hard decisions in order to fulfill your Master Plan of financial freedom.

> *Leave it up to me while I be livin' proof*
> *To kick the truth to the young Black youth.*
> **C.R.E.A.M. by Wu Tang Clan**

The truth of the matter is you need a plan! Let's take a look at your current expenses again. At this stage of your plan, you have what you have. In other words, your income is your income and your expenses are your expenses. Are there any areas on your current expenses that you can target that will benefit you in the long run? I am sure there are. You must go line-by-line and check to see if reductions could be made to any of your outstanding debts. The first thing to look at would be student loans. According to the site CNBC.com, over 44 million Americans have student loan debt that exceeds over $1.5 TRILLION. These obligations are not going anywhere and will be with you for the long haul. We are going to concentrate on paying them off, but not immediately. We will leverage these debts with the options that we have available and begin to work on our budget. Begin by contacting your student loan servicer and finding out if a deferment or forbearance on your account is possible. If you can get this approved for 12 months, you can use the money allocated for these payments to cut down your credit card debt and not affect your budget or your credit score. Deferments and forbearances freeze your required payments, but in most cases, additional interest is still accrued. That's an acceptable tradeoff when considering our ultimate goal.

Next you will target your communications budget. The average cell phone bill for users of smartphones is $80.25 per line due to the recent practice of leasing phones. That extrapolates to over $400 per month for a family of 5. Are there any reductions that can be gained on your current cell plan? Can you pay off any of your devices to reduce your monthly outlay of income? Due to the competitive nature of the cellular industry, consider other carriers as a way of decreasing your monthly bill. How about your home cable/internet/phone plan? Most of the time cable companies want to lock you in by offering "bundles" on their services. They will tell you that getting all of the services that they offer will cost you less in the long run due to this bundle practice. If you truly use all of these services, that may actually be the case. But how many of you actually *still* use your home phone? How many of those 400 television stations do you actually watch? And can you really tell the difference between 100 Mbps and 400 Mbps? Better yet, do you even know what it means? Depending on your usage, most will not be able to determine the difference between the speeds. Take the time to compare your current plan with other available options. Most that do compare find that they are able to save over $100 per month on the services they normally use versus what they pay for monthly. Whatever the savings, you can target your credit cards even more and get those payments erased faster. Your mortgage/rent, car note, and insurances will actually be considered as a group. Should you downsize your home? Should you trade in your car(s) and get something with lower payments? Should you consider leasing over buying? Should you search for other insurance options to lower costs? These are always difficult choices, but ones that could save you hundreds per month on your home and autos. Your goal for doing all of this is to get back to zero so that you can begin building your CREAM. With the newfound riches gained from these budget adjustments, you can begin the plan of targeting your debt.

> *That charge of energy set all the Carters back*
> *It took all these years to get to zero in fact*
> **Legacy by Jay-Z**

Your first target will be your outstanding credit card debt. Start by using your new monthly savings to pay off your credit card debt. Issuers of credit cards classify its account holders into two categories: "transactors" – those who use credit cards for purchases and pay the balance each month, and "revolvers" – those who carry a balance over from month to month, usually paying only the minimum payment that is due. Almost forty percent of all credit card users are revolvers. If you were to continue to pay the minimum amounts due on your credit cards, it would take ten years and one month to eliminate your credit card debt. Ten years!!! By targeting credit card debt with the freed-up money, you will be able to pay off your debt in a fairly short period of time. But paying off the credit card debt is not the end of the story. You must RESIST the continued use of these cards. You must be COMMITED to not running the balances on the cards up again! Remember "Cash Rules," not credit.

If required, use your newly generated cash influx to make a necessary purchase, not your credit. This plan also works in conjunction with increasing your credit score. Paying off your credit card debt will reduce your utilization, thereby possibly increasing your score. You want to pay off the credit card accounts, but not close them. You want the creditors to continue to report the payment history on the account each month as well as the new balance. Each month the account balance is zero, the creditors will report as if a payment were made. Once you have paid off your credit cards, you will free up even more money to then target your auto loans.

You will take the combined budgeted funds allocated for student loans and credit cards and redirect them to your auto loan. This will allow you to pay off the auto loans much faster than your contract requires. Once the auto loan is paid, you will begin the task of paying off your student loans. In June of 2018, Forbes Magazine reported that of the 44.2 million people that owed student loan debt, the average amount owed was about $38,400 per person repaid in about 10 years.[18] That is a long time to pay for your education. If you continue to redirect your original student loan payment amount, along with the savings from credit card and auto loans, you can eliminate your student loan debt very quickly and then begin the process of saving. It will take some time, but if you continue this targeted plan to pay off your debt, you will get to zero much faster than you think.

In every step of this targeting plan, you have to make sure you keep very good records of your progress to make sure you are maximizing your efforts. If the technology suggestion of software such as QuickBooks is too daunting, go old school. Write everything in a notebook and keep a checkbook ledger. You want to ALWAYS be aware of your spending. As there is not such thing as a perfect plan, you must always be willing to alter course if an emergency arises or if a more efficient and winnable scenario presents itself. The most important thing is that you win in your efforts to eliminate your debt.

All I do is win win win no matter what,
Got money on my mind I can never get enough!
All I Do Is Win by DJ Khaled

CHAPTER 3 HOT TAKES

1. The word "Budget" is not a bad word. A budget is created so that we can hold on to our assets.

2. Develop your budget to spend AT MOST 70% of your income on expenses and save AT LEAST 30% of your income for investments.

3. Utilize technology to keep track of all of your finances. This includes a budget and a banking application.

4. Remember this if nothing else: It is NEVER TOO LATE to start saving!

5. Begin to use Targeted Payments as a way of reducing your debt.

6. The ultimate goal for our budget and our finances is to GET BACK TO ZERO!!!

ELIMINATING HARD TIMES

CHAPTER FOUR

CHAPTER 4 – ELIMINATING

HARD TIMES

H ip-Hop, as a musical genre and as a culture, has been mocked, shunned, and at times considered a musically inferior art form following its introduction to the world in the 1970's. It was considered an inner-city fad and was looked upon as the bastard stepchild of the music world. Who would have thought that the "revolution" started by DJ Kool Herc, a teenage Jamaican born DJ living in west Bronx, New York, would become the phenomenon that is Hip-Hop. Today Hip-Hop can be heard in mainstream advertising, professional sporting events, movie scores, and just about anywhere else music is played. Hip-Hop has proven worthy of the same types of accolades given to other music genres such as Rock, Country, R&B, Jazz and more. In fact, the Rock & Roll Hall of Fame in Cleveland, Ohio is another example of how Hip-Hop has transcended popular culture. The Hall is dedicated to archiving the history of some of the most influential artists, producers, engineers and others who have left a lasting impression on the world of music. In 2007, the Rock & Roll Hall of Fame accepted the genius of Hip-Hop and inducted its first members in Grand Master Flash and the Furious Five. *"It's like a jungle sometimes, it makes me wonder how I keep from going under"* was the hook for the iconic **The Message**, a track that brought Hip-Hop into the social conscience of America. Two years later in 2009, the Rock & Roll Hall of Fame also recognized the gifts given to us by Run D.M.C.

> *Hard Times spreading just like the flu*
> *Watch out homeboy don't let it catch you.*
> *P-p-p-prices go up, don't let your pockets go down*
> *When you got short money you're stuck on the ground.*
>
> **Hard Times by Run D.M.C.**

These lyrics are taken from the first track of the 1983 debut album for Run D.M.C. As a 14-year-old boy growing up in the hood, *Hard Times* served as an anthem for what we were going through and a rallying cry to *"keep (our) eye on the prize."*

Everyone goes through some form of hard times in his or her life. It would not be called *life* if you did not experience some trials and some tribulations. Even those that have gained various measures of success have experienced hard times. Bill Gates, the founder of Microsoft said, "Success is as fleeting as life itself, it can all be taken away at a moment's notice. Nothing is permanent. The only constant in life is change."[19] This is especially true when it comes to your financial security. We may find success with our finances, but if we become complacent or satisfied, our successes could be taken away from us at the drop of a dime. Experiencing hard times does not necessarily mean that you are struggling to make ends meet. Even the richest of the rich have experienced hard times in one form or another. Milton Hershey failed miserably with three different companies before he finally perfected the tasty milk chocolate that we love today. Theodor Giesel had his manuscripts described as "pure rubbish" and rejected by 27 publishers before finally running into an old friend that had just become a children's literature editor. Today you know Theodor as Dr. Seuss. Thomas Edison failed several *thousand* times in his attempt to make a light bulb. When he finally succeeded, he stated, "I have not failed. I've just found 10,000 ways that won't work." Walt Disney, who began his career in newspapers, was fired from his job for not being creative enough. His Mickey Mouse cartoons were rejected and deemed too scary for women. Today his estate is valued at more than $5 billion. How is that for creativity? Michael Jordan was cut from his high school basketball team and overlooked by several college scouts because he was considered too short and not good enough to play college basketball. After a career that saw him win an NCAA basketball championship, lead the NBA in scoring 10 times (7 consecutive), win 6 NBA championships, 5 League MVP's, and 6 NBA Finals MVP's, Jordan was voted as the greatest North American athlete of the 20th Century by ESPN in 1999. As a cherry-on-top, Jordan has amassed a personal net worth of over $1.31 billion from his many business ventures. Take that Laney High School! These are just a few people that have experienced some sort of hard times prior to them becoming the success stories that we know today. These are well-known examples, but you can find thousands that are similar yet unknown. Your story could be the next one on this list. You may have experienced hard times financially in the past. Your credit history may have been a little bruised, and your budget may have been out of whack, but I am here to tell you that there is hope.

After working so diligently to build an excellent credit history and getting your debt back to zero, it is now time to create the type of income that will allow you to live life and not just survive it. A scene in the 20th Century Fox movie *The Martian* saw astronaut Mark Watney discussing his hard times while stranded alone on Mars. "At some point, everything's gonna go south on you and you're going to say, this is it. This is how I end. Now you can either accept that, or you can get to work. That's all it is. You just begin. You do the math. You solve one problem, and then the next one, and then the next. And if you solve enough problems, you get to come home."[20] This advice works if you are stuck on Mars alone or if you are stuck in the mundane of living check to check. You do the math. You solve each problem one by one and if you solve enough of your financial problems, you came come home to financial freedom. Right now, the math is just not adding up. You have created some breathing room with your budget adjustments, but those adjustments alone will not suffice to fulfill your stated goal of financial freedom. At the end of the day, you need more income.

THE TAX BRACKETS

In the United States, we live in a capitalistic society characterized by free markets where individuals or businesses own the capital goods and supply and demand dictate the production of goods or services. Although very, very far from a perfect economy, it does allow an opportunity for someone that is not averse to taking risks to become rewarded for their efforts. Some of my most heated debates are with my best friend as we discuss the merits of capitalism and its many pitfalls. I am for capitalism as it provides an opportunity for everyone to create his or her own wealth, whereas he is against it because it invariably creates inequalities of income and wealth. Due to the fact that the means of production are directly in the hands of individuals or businesses, the producers not only acquire a disproportionately larger amount of the income, they also have the power to suppress the earning potential of their employees. This allows for a very large portion of the wealth to be acquired by a very small percentage of the population. In laymen's terms, capitalism creates different tax brackets. As evident by the 2014 tax returns filed in the United States, there are seven different tax brackets in this country[21]:

Tax Rate	Single Filers	Married Filers	Head of Household Filers
10%	$0 to $9,275 *# of Returns* **(34,058,969)**	$0 to $18,550 *# of Returns* **(16,402,401)**	$0 to $13,250 *# of Returns* **(14,203,510)**
15%	$9,275 to $37,650 *# of Returns* **(22,547,469)**	$18,550 to $75,300 *# of Returns* **(22,234,309)**	$13,250 to $50,400 *# of Returns* **(6,065,538)**
25%	$37,650 to $91,150 *# of Returns* **(10,706,456)**	$75,300 to $151,900 *# of Returns* **(12,667,232)**	$50,400 to $130,150 *# of Returns* **(1,600,377)**
28%	$91,150 to $190,150 *# of Returns* **(1,820,584)**	$151,900 to $231,450 *# of Returns* **(3,092,037)**	$130,150 to $210,800 *# of Returns* **(125,699)**
33%	$190,150 to $413,350 *# of Returns* **(334,409)**	$231,450 to $413,350 *# of Returns* **(1,524,157)**	$210,800 to $413,350 *# of Returns* **(53,576)**
35%	$413,350 to $415,050 *# of Returns* **(973)**	$413,350 to $466,950 *# of Returns* **(185,137)**	$413,350 to $441,000 *# of Returns* **(3,837)**
39.6%	$415,050+ *# of Returns* **(110,722)**	$466,950+ *# of Returns* **(843,217)**	$441,000+ *# of Returns* **(24,961)**

Combined, there were 148,606,578 tax returns filed for the 2014 Tax Year with reported adjustable gross income of over $9.77 trillion. A closer look at this 2014 Tax Year will give us the following data:

TAX BRACKET	# OF FILED RETURNS	TOTAL ADJUSTED GROSS INCOME (In Thousands)	MEDIAN ADJUSTED GROSS INCOME PER BRACKET
10 Percent	64,665,888	$836,693,508	$12,938.72
15 Percent	50,847,316	$2,938,231,395	$57,785.38
25 Percent	24,974,065	$2,670,701,271	$106,938.99
28 Percent	5,038,320	$1,007,696,408	$200,006.43
33 Percent	1,912,142	$692,255,055	$362,031.20
35 Percent	189,947	$101,093,946	$532,221.86
39.6 Percent	978,900	$1,524,363,828	$1,557,221.20
TOTALS	148,606,578	$9,771,035,412	$65,751.03

So what does this data tell us? The answer is a lot! The first thing we recognize is that only about .78% of the tax filers in the US have a median adjusted gross income above $500,000. That is a little more than ¾ of 1 percent. Another point to notice is the combined median adjusted gross income of the first six tax brackets ($1,271,923) is less than the median adjusted gross income of the highest tax bracket ($1,577,221). I told you that this is not a book about stats and charts, but rather it is a book about planning. We need this data to continue with our planning. Which tax bracket would you fall under? Don't be ashamed of your current level. You will soon develop plans that will "Move You On Up" like the Jeffersons. Just think about it for a second.

As stated before, Hard Times are a result of living. If you are living, you will continue to experience Hard Times. You will constantly be faced with situations that will test your resolve and make you question if what you are doing is worth it. But I would rather take another approach towards Hard Times. Where others see setbacks, I see opportunities. I am pretty certain that if you are reading this book, you have experienced setbacks in your financial life and are looking for ideas on how to overcome those setbacks. I talked about tax brackets because of two reasons. The first reason is to get you thinking about how you want to live your life and the second reason is to point out that taxes in theory are a good thing (and I know that sounds crazy, but just think about it for a second). I asked you to boastfully say which tax bracket your current income falls under.

If you are like most Americans, you are in the 25 percent tax bracket. This means that if you are an employee, the income created from fifteen minutes of every hour that you work goes to Uncle Sam. It doesn't sound like much but think of it this way – for every eight-hour work shift, two hours of your work income goes to the government BEFORE you ever get to see a penny of your income. That is a little more concerning. But wait there is more! How about the fact that 520

hours of a typical employee's income will be used to pay their taxes. That

equates to 65 days of working for free to pay your IRS bill. Think about

that for a second…let it marinate with you just a little longer! You are

working for over two months out of the year for free. Now that *does not*

sound like fun. But what is my solution for you? BE HAPPY TO PAY

EVEN MORE TAXES!!! Paying taxes is a good thing. Yes I said that!

I would love to pay $1,000,000 in taxes. Why? Because if I am paying

that amount in taxes, that means my income for the year was over $2.5

million…and probably way over that amount based on taxable income

reductions. I feel very confident that I could survive on $1.5 million

after paying all of my tax liabilities. I mean VERY confident! Now please

do not think for a second that I do not want to reduce my tax liability as

much as possible with as many of the reduction methods made available

to me by the IRS tax codes. I want to pay the least amount of taxes just

like any other proud American – just ask Trump how that works. Well,

maybe I won't go as far as 45 when it comes to creative accounting

methods, but I do want to LEGALLY save as much of my income as

possible.

OVERCOMING THE HARD TIMES

Overcoming Hard Times is a daily fight and you must stay on top of your game to combat obstacles both seen and unseen. You have your stated goal of financial freedom and you have started down that road, but you are going to need to do a lot more in order to attain your goal. If you are in the 25 percent tax bracket, there is a high probability your income is a result of an employer paying you for your services to their company. That is fine and has worked for you up until this point. The only problem with working FOR someone is that you are never in control of your earning potential. The chances of you becoming financially independent are very unlikely if you are an employee because your earning potential will always be restricted. **SCREAMING FROM THE TOP OF MY LUNGS:** *"I am not telling you to quit your job and become self-employed!!!"* What I am asking you to do is consider adding additional sources of income into your portfolio. The more sources of income you have, the less likely your Hard Times will become overwhelming. For anyone that values financial security or desires financial freedom, generating additional sources of income is not a recommendation but rather a necessity. Diversifying your income is also the best way to avoid Hard Times.

There are two types of income – active income and passive income. Active income is generated as a result of your work...your sweat. This can include any income generated from a "normal" job, a business that you have an active participation, tips, and bonuses. Passive income is generated as a result of little or no effort on your part. This can include dividend income, interest income, rental income, and royalties. If you search the internet for the best way to become a millionaire, you will find that most books, bloggers, financial gurus and the such will tell you that generating several sources of income is the best way to attain your goal. Most will tell you that the magic number is seven, but I disagree. I think that the magic number is ten. Why ten? I am so glad you asked. I am a fan of an older crime drama series that ran from 2002 until 2009 called *Monk* starring Tony Shalhoub. In this series, Adrian Monk was a brilliant detective with the San Francisco Police Department until his wife Trudy was killed in a car-bombing incident. After the incident, Monk began working as a consultant solving crimes and bringing justice to the victims. Monk suffered from obsessive-compulsive disorder

(OCD) and had to have everything perfect and numbers round in order to survive. Well, I am the same. Seven is the number for completion in the biblical sense, but it is not round. Ten is a round number. In order to be perfectly free from all of your debts and gain perfect financial freedom, you must develop the perfect amount of income sources and that perfect number in THIS book is ten. From these two types of income come seven income streams:

1. **Earned Income** – Active income earned by doing something or working for someone.
2. **Profit** – Active income earned by selling something for more than it costs you to make.
3. **Interest** – Passive income earned as a result of lending your money to someone else to use.
4. **Dividend Income** – Passive income earned as a return on shares of a company you own.
5. **Rental Income** – Passive income earned as a result of renting out an asset that you own.
6. **Capital Gains** – Passive income earned as a result of increase in value of an asset that you own.
7. **Royalties** – Passive income earned as a result of letting someone use your products, ideas, or processes.

Now let's try to figure out how we are going to get ten sources out of these seven streams.

Everything in this book is connected and I keep restating our past efforts. This is because you need to make sure you are constantly trying to work your plan. In step one, we made sure that our credit history was corrected of any prior issues. In step two, we realized that our month was longer than our money and devised a plan that would target our debts in an attempt to pay them off earlier and begin our trip down the road to financial freedom. Now we have come to step three where we are trying to overcome our Hard Times and create more income. If you are like most, you only have an earned income source. This source has allowed you to provide the necessities for your family but not establish enough savings for emergencies or retirement. Since you are this far in the book, I can only assume that you have been following along and creating your own plan. By now you realize that your single income source is not going to be enough to satisfy your kindred goal.

Let's say for the sake of argument that you are 50 years old and would like to have a net worth of at least $1,000,000 upon your retirement in 10 years. You have followed your plan and have gotten back to zero, but ZERO also is the state of your savings account. This example seems laughable because surely you would have saved some money by the age of 50. Shockingly, according to a 2015 analysis done by the federal government, this is a fate suffered by over 30% of the US population. But thankfully, it is not too late to create our wealth and enjoy a wonderful retirement. The objective is to generate a net worth of at least $1,000,000 within ten years. As Mark Watney said, let's just do the math. This amounts to generating a minimum of $100,000 net worth each year for the next 10 years or $8,333.33 each month for the next 120 months. Daunting yes, but not nearly impossible. So how you can create this additional income each month? Let's break it down.

Tryin' to get my hands on some Grants like Horace
All About the Benjamins by P. Diddy

CHAPTER 4 HOT TAKES

1. Everyone faces Hard Times. Nothing is permanent. The only constant in life is change.

2. A little more than ¾ of 1 percent of the American taxpayers make more than $500,000 per year.

3. Answer this question for yourself: "How do YOU want to live your life?"

4. Overcoming Hard Times is a DAILY fight. Stay dedicated to the battle.

5. Think about generating passive income from the seven identified streams of income.

THE
10
SOURCES

—

CHAPTER FIVE

CHAPTER 5 – THE 10 SOURCES

I remember growing up in East St. Louis, Illinois and always talking with my boys about how we all wanted to become rich. We wanted the fine luxury cars, the magnificent mansions, the iced-out jewelry, and the finest clothes that we could find. We would constantly daydream about what life would be like if New Edition hadn't stolen our act. It should have been *US* instead of Ronnie, Bobby, Ricky, Mike and Ralph onstage with all of those adoring fans and royalty checks. Unlike NE, we were never discovered so our chances to become rich faded. Being rich has driven a lot of people, but rich is not what you want to be. For most people, being rich means you make a lot of money. That may be true, but most rich people also spend a lot of money. "Rich folk" overspend their money in a way many would consider frivolous – on "toys" rather than assets. Thinking back over our daydreams, I see that had we become "rich," we would have spent our fortunes on a lot of things that would not have increased our worth either, just like the other rich people. Typically, people that are considered rich tend to make purchasing decisions without thinking about the ramifications to their overall net worth. Sometimes "rich folk" live check to check and have a mountain of debt that is overwhelming too. In the long run, it doesn't really matter much if you are making $300,000 per year if you are spending $285,000. You would be better off if you made $60,000 and spent $30,000. Being rich can be nice, but being wealthy is a lot better. Sometimes we want to confuse being rich with being wealthy. The truth of the matter is that they are two ENTIRELY different situations. Wealthy people accumulate assets, have very little debt, have a nice savings nest egg, and live well within their means. You have begun your path to accumulating wealth; you just don't realize it yet. You have eliminated your debt and reduced your expenses to begin living more within you means. That's half of the wealthy formula. Now it's time to accumulate assets and generate a nice nest egg.

> *Now I have a seat at my table, let me do you the business*
> *Diversify your millions, you can live off the interest*
> *Make every revenue stream flood, see where it took me*
> *And make that money stack higher than giraffe's (you see)**
> **Everything by Xzibit**

In the reality that is your financial portfolio, the ultimate goal is to get into the 39.6% tax bracket – or as some would say it, become a millionaire (39.6 club). Yes, it sounds very good to say *I am a millionaire*, but it feels even better when you can look into your personal portfolio and see the proof. Not only do you want to become a millionaire, you want to become a WEALTHY millionaire. To attain this goal, you need to mimic other wealthy millionaires. It goes without saying that most millionaires have several sources of income generating their enormous fortunes. They know that the more revenue streams they possess, the better their balance sheet will look. They learned that it is never a good idea to rely on a single income source, so they diversified their portfolios thereby enhancing their chances for success and reducing their chances of failure. It's just that simple. Like Watney, they have done the math and determined that the probability of failure is much less with several sources than with one. If you dedicate yourself to trying to generate income from ten different sources, you will be able to continue to thrive even if four of them are slow or not producing as well as you would like. You will still have the remaining six sources working in your favor. There will always be differences between everyone's plan. You will need to tailor your plan to fit your particular situation. As you develop your plan and your portfolio, there will always be certain aspects that encourage you about your plan and other aspects that leave you a little less encouraged.

The key is to allocate more resources to the encouraging portions of your portfolio and to alter or reconsider the direction of the less encouraging portions. Growing up in a traditional Baptist church in the Midwest, one rule we would live by was things are *always* subject to change. The same thing could be said when discussing finances. When you develop your plan, remember that it is a blueprint of how you would like your financial history to look. But take note, no matter how carefully a plan is crafted, something could still go wrong. As Robert Burns wrote in 1786, "The best laid schemes of mice and men often go awry." In other words, even the best plan of action has the potential of messing up. You must think of *all* of the possible pros and cons of the decisions you make regarding your portfolio DAILY. How many times a day do you check your banking app or bank website? I am constantly checking my app to see what is going on with my accounts. It has become second nature now. I even have text message notifications whenever there are ANY transactions conducted on my accounts. It can become tedious with all of the messages. But believe me when I say it is better than the alternative when you miss a transaction or there is something that is unauthorized. You need to make it a habit to routinely check all of your financial accounts.

This idea of different sources of income is as old as wealth itself. Even though McDonald's sells hamburgers, they have been involved in several other businesses since their opening in 1940. Did you know that McDonald's developed the concept of Redbox in 2002? The self-serve video rental station positioned at gas stations, grocery stores, drug stores, and of course, McDonald's restaurants provided a lucrative stream of income for the corporation until they sold the rights in 2009. The corporation also owned Donata's Pizza (until 2003), Chipotle Mexican Grill (until 2006), and Boston Market (until 2007). Currently they still own Krispy Kreme Donuts, Millie's Cookies, Dairy Queen, and Panera Bread to name a few. In 2016 McDonalds earned $6 billion including $3.6 billion from company owned restaurants and another $2.4 billion from franchise income. There are three lessons to be learned from McDonalds: diversify, diversify, and diversify.

MAKE EVERY BEAT MATTER

Most people average 2.21 billion heartbeats in their lifetime. If you consider that there are 60 beats per minute, this gives you about 70 years in this world. In other words, EACH BEAT MATTERS!!! How many have you wasted already? This question is not looking for an answer, it's just meant as a statement to make you think. The time to think about this is now. So let's think! If we do some additional math and break down our goal just a little further, we will see that the $100,000 we need each year equates to $48.08 per hour using the standard 40-hour workweek. Rounding that number to $50.00, let's think about how we can generate an additional $50 per hour? Grab a notebook and begin jotting down different ideas to use as your guide to figure this question out. What are some of the things that you enjoy doing? Are you a foodie? A workout warrior? A crafty person? How about a designer? Write down all of the different things you like doing and things you like buying. Most of the time, we are our own source of inspiration and don't even realize it. Personally I like building stuff. I was never trained to build; I just started doing it because I enjoyed seeing the things that I created. I can extrapolate this joy of building into a desire to get into real estate. Of the top 10 ways most Americans become millionaires, real estate is number eight. The complete list includes Investments, Technology, Media, Energy, Food & Beverage, Service, Fashion & Retail, Manufacturing, and Sports. Off the top, I can eliminate sports from my own personal list. I am pretty confident that ship has sailed…unless of course my golf game takes off and I make the Seniors Tour (or whatever they call it right now). Referring back to the list that you just wrote down, I am fairly certain that most of the things you listed can be associated to one of these categories.

Real estate to me was both rewarding and lucrative. It was one of the things on my list as well as a lot of other people. There is great joy in finding a home that just needs a little tender loving care, restoring its beauty, and selling it to a family that will share thousands of memories there; while at the same time receiving a check at closing that will put a smile on YOUR face. As with most businesses, you want to purchase or build a product at a low price and sell the product for a profit. This is how you create wealth. If you are like most, you have watched any number of programs on television or online where different people are telling you of the millions of dollars you can make in real estate. A lot of

CHAPTER 5 – THE 10 SOURCES

them will tell you that it can be done with little or none of your own money. Just send $99.99 plus shipping and handling and they will tell you all of the "secrets" of real estate. Well, let me tell you a little secret...all you are really doing is contributing to THEIR ability to get into the 39.6 club. Is it possible to buy real estate this way? As Kevin Garnett said after winning the 2008 NBA Championship with the Boston Celtics, "Anything is Possible!!!" My addendum would just include, "But not probable." If buying real estate with little or no money down were as easy as they would like to make it out to be, EVERYONE would be doing it. The "No Money Down" premise involves finding distressed properties, tying it up with a contract for an extended period of time, finding a buyer for the property, and then selling it to make a profit. But why would the homeowner agree to that? Why would they allow you to sell their home and make a huge profit on THEIR home? But desperation can make people do crazy things. I have been in that state of desperation before, so I understand. I am a PRAYER...just not a PREYER! It is entirely possible to find someone in this situation, and it is also possible that they would agree to a contract like the one suggested. But it is certain that the only person that makes consistent money from this technique is the person that sold you the "Get Rich Quick in Real Estate" book. There are tons of other ways to make your millions in real estate without becoming a "wolf." There are tax lien certificates, tax deed sales, bank REO properties, and properties that are listed below market that just need help or refurbishing.

REAL ESTATE RAMBLINGS

Tax lien certificates have fast become the favorite avenue for a lot of investors. In order for cities and counties to offer its residents vital services such as waste removal, hospital services, police enforcement, and schools, taxes are levied on property owners in an attempt to cover the cost of these expenses. As a matter of practice, a lien is placed on every property for the amount of the taxes due each year. The budget for these municipalities is determined based on the tax base for the area. If everyone pays their taxes as required, the municipalities can offer much better services. But the truth of the matter is nothing is 100%. You will never find that 100% of the population paid their taxes on time, if at all. So what are the remedies for the municipalities when someone does not pay their required taxes? One such remedy is offering the tax lien that is placed on every property for sale on an open market to cover the budget shortfall from the uncollected taxes. These tax liens supersede any other liens including a current mortgage. For example, lets assume that John is unable to pay his $2,500 tax bill for the current tax season. The municipality has already allocated John's payment when determining their budget for the year and therefore need the monies due. After several unsuccessful attempts to collect on the taxes from John, the municipality will have no recourse other than to offer John's tax lien for sale to investors at a Tax Auction. As an investment, this is a great opportunity for a decent return. Depending on the guidelines of the municipality, a delinquency penalty would be assessed to John at an annual rate between 12% and 24% for his non-payment. As an investor, a minimum 12% rate of return is in line with the average rate of return on common mutual funds. It is especially good considering the low interest rates being offered now on Certificates of Deposit and municipal bonds. This is a win for the municipalities because by selling the tax liens, they are able to cover budget shortfall caused by John's inability to pay his required taxes. This is a win for the investor because they will receive an increase on their investment of at least 12% with potentially more if the current homeowner cannot repay the tax lien. Depending on the municipality, the owner of the tax lien could possibly foreclose on the property and become the new owner if the lien is not repaid. This is not the norm for these types of investments, but it is a possibility.

Tax deed sales are a great way to purchase real estate at below market values. Tax deeds are properties that have already been foreclosed by the county or state where they are located for non-payment of tax liabilities. The municipality will then sell the property at auction to recover the monies owed by the previous owner. These properties are usually without any liens and are offered at auction for the amount of taxes owed plus applicable fees and interest charges. The length of the time for delinquency before foreclosure varies from state to state, but most will range from one year to three years before foreclosure proceedings are initiated. This option for purchasing real estate requires a GREAT amount of due diligence considering you will be purchasing most of these properties site unseen. You must be aware of the risks as well as the potential for great reward when considering purchasing one of these properties.

Another great source of income from real estate comes from what is more commonly known as "flipping." If you turn on the television to the HGTV Network, DIY Network, or A&E, you will find shows such as Flip or Flop, Masters of Flip, or Flipping Las Vegas just to name a few. These are different shows on different networks, but with the same goal in mind – to purchase a home at a below market cost, invest in improvements, and sell it for a profit. According to Time magazine, 2016 marked the high in the number of people attempting to get into the flipping business since 2007 when the housing market crashed. Why? Because the average profit during the first quarter of 2016 was $58,520. This is why you can turn on the TV and see a *ton* of home improvement and flipping shows. You can even find them on demand. But be warned. It is not as easy as it may look on television. To wake up one day and decide that you want to become a house flipper is very dangerous. If you are not careful, you can lose a large portion of your portfolio attempting to flip a house. The key to this source of real estate income is a ton...I mean a **TON** of research. You must spend an insane amount of time searching different sources for the perfect flip candidate. Contact a realtor, look through different newspapers, search online, do a drive-by in a targeted neighborhood. The more research that you do, the better your chances of being successful with flipping. Once you find the right property, you will then need to spend even more time coordinating the transformation of the property into a home a buyer will fall in love with and a property that will sell very fast. It is a very rewarding process when handled correctly. But that is just it. The biggest issue with flipping houses is that the process is sometimes not handled correctly. Many investors forget to consider or just don't know all of the anticipated costs for their project. But if you know the pitfalls and plan accordingly, flipping houses can become a great source of income.

BUILDING THE 10 SOURCES

Real estate is just one additional source of income. It can either be an active or passive source. As we continue to build our List of 10, we need to consider other sources as well. As previously mentioned, investments are the number one source of income for most millionaires and everyone should have some type of investment account. There are three main types of investments, each with differing levels of risk: stocks, bonds, and mutual funds. A stock is an investment in a specific company. When you purchase a stock, you are buying a small share of the company's earnings and assets. The value of a stock fluctuates minute-by-minute depending on the strength of the business.

Companies sell their stock to raise money for their business. Investors buy and sell these stocks, sometimes at a profit, sometimes at a loss. Stocks are your typical High Risk, High Reward investment. You have the ability to earn more money, possibly at a much faster pace than other investments. But be warned! You can also lose your shirt in a matter of minutes. Stocks are not for the faint of heart; but for the aggressive investor, they could create enormous earning potential.

Bonds are a loan to a company or a government. When you purchase a bond, you are in effect giving the bond issuer a loan to use for their corporation or their government. As a return, the issuer will pay you interest for allowing them to use your money. Bonds usually have lower risks than stocks, so the return rate is usually lower. As with any loan, the negative is the possibility of a loan default. US Government bonds are backed by the "full faith and credit" of the United States. They are considered virtually the safest investment available. State and local government bonds are considered the next safest, followed by corporate bonds. When you buy a bond, you agree to loan money to the bond issuer for a set amount of time. The issuer pays the interest usually once or twice a year and the principal amount of the loan on the maturity date.

The maturity date is set when you purchase the bond. As an example, if you purchased a 10-year US Treasury bond (a minimum of $1,000 denomination) at a rate of return of 1.732%, you will receive semi-annual interest payments in the amount of $17.32 per $1,000 bond. If we do the math for ten years, you will receive $346.40 in interest throughout the ten years plus the principal amount will mature at the end of the term. By definition, this is an investment. I am just not so sure it is a good investment...JUST MY PERSONAL OPINION.

A mutual fund is an investment that is designed to pool the money from several investors in an effort to purchase a collection of stocks, bonds, and other securities. The fund has a management company that decides what securities to purchase and how best to utilizing the pool of money to create a greater level of diversification. Mutual funds are traded on the stock exchange just as stocks are traded. There are different types of funds with differing degrees of risk and expected rates of return. Mutual funds are similar to our idea of The 10. They invest in several different stocks and securities so if one is faltering, the others will pick it up minimalizing the risk of losing money. The risk level for mutual funds depends on the type of fund you are investing and the management company that you utilize. The average rate of return on investment for all mutual funds is about 8%, thereby making them a very solid investment.

Everyone needs to invest his or her money into some form of investment account. Even little investments over time can create life-changing income. Let's say you are the proud parent or grandparent of a newborn baby. If you were to invest $1 per day or $365 per year for 21 years into a mutual fund that pays compound interest and opt to reinvest the interest earned, the mutual fund account could have over $1 million when the child goes to retire at age 65. Think about that for a second. A total of about $7,700 invested into an account could allow the child to retire a millionaire (based on 8% rate of return). That is how Legacy Wealth is created. If we were to encourage our families to establish a mutual fund account for all of our children and do this very simple thing, none of our children would have to worry about living a life full of financial worry ever again.

But what exactly is compound interest? Compound interest is "interest on interest." In other words, it is interest that is earned on an investment and then reinvested to earn even more interest. Simple interest is just interest that is earned on the principle amount invested only. For example, a $10,000 investment creating 10% simple interest will be worth $15,000 in five years. The same investment creating 10% interest compounded annually will be worth $16,105 in five years. The account distributing compound interest created an additional $1,105 in value in the same 5-year period. Now for the even better news: interest can be compounded annually, semi-annually, quarterly, monthly, or even DAILY. The more times the interest is compounded, the more money the fund will generate. As with any investment, you want to do a TON of research before deciding on which fund to invest. The main thing to understand in this matter is you MUST invest in some type of investment fund. This is passive income at its finest and will be significantly counted on as one of your 10. But those are just a few sources. What else can you do to create more passive income? The following list will give you some examples of passive income:

- Create a YouTube video channel and utilize Google AdSense
- Use your blog or website to promote products from affiliates
- Write and promote an eBook
- Invest in Energy
- Maintain vending and ATM machines

- Create a music channel on SoundCloud, Vimeo, or YouTube

- Establish a Coaching or Consulting Business

- Develop an online course

- Create websites that will drive traffic to other sellers

Now this is not an all-inclusive list, but it is a starting point for you to think about how to create your 10 Streams of Income. Remember, it is our plan to generate $50 per hour. How easy would it be for you to create $5 per hour from 10 sources? You will be in the 39.6 club in no time!

Financial freedom my only hope
F*ck livin' rich and dyin' broke
I bought some artwork for 1 million
2 years later, that sh*t worth 2 million
Few years later, that sh*t worth 8 million
I can't wait to give this sh*t to my children
Y'all think it's bougie, I'm like, it's fine
But I'm tryin' to give you a million
dollars worth of game for $9.99

The Story of O.J. by Jay-Z

CHAPTER 5 HOT TAKES

1. It is much better to become wealthy than to become rich.

2. Our goal should be to become a member of the 39.6 Club.

3. The whole purpose of "The 10" is to significantly reduce the risk of Hard Times by increasing the number of income streams we generate; thereby decreasing the probability of a financial failure.

4. Always remember this: Plans are always subject to change…especially financial plans.

5. Most people average 2.21 billion heartbeats in our lives. Make every single one count!!!

6. Most of the time we are our own source of inspiration.

7. You MUST invest in some type of investment fund.

8. Compound interest is our BEST friend.

PROTECT YOUR NECK

CHAPTER SIX

CHAPTER 6 – PROTECT YOUR NECK

I magine this is the year 1992 and we are in the borough of Staten Island in New York City. As we walk down the streets, we can hear the sounds of The Pharcyde's *Passin' Me By*, Das Efx's *Mic Checka*, and CL Smooth's *They Reminisce Over You*. Hip-Hop could be heard everywhere. You had sounds of groups like GangStarr, the Beastie Boys, and House of Pain emanating from all over. It was becoming the charge for all urban youth. Hip-Hop was king! In 1992, Robert Diggs, known today as RZA, was a fledging artist who had just been released from his recording contract with Tommy Boy Records. He began collaborating with Dennis Coles, more commonly known as the Ghostface Killa. Together they decided to create a new rap group whose style would be a cross between Eastern philosophy Kung Fu movies and the Five Percent Nation whose teachings they picked up off the New York streets. In late 1992 they joined with RZA's cousin Gary Grice, A.K.A. the GZA, and Russell Jones, the ever-popular Ol' Dirty Bastard

(ODB), to create one of Hip-Hop's most historic groups, The Wu-Tang Clan, with RZA being the de facto leader and music producer. The group enlisted the services of U-God, Method Man, Raekwon the Chef, and Inspectah Deck to record its first single released in December of 1992 – *Protect Your Neck*. Because both RZA and GZA had previous record deals that did not give them the type of residuals that they thought they deserved, the Wu, as they are affectionately, called released the song as a form of protest.

> *The Wu is too slamming for these Cold Killing labels*
> *Some ain't had hits since I seen Aunt Mabel*
> *Be doing artists in like Cain did Abel*
> *Now they money's gettin stuck to the gum under the table*
> **Protect Your Neck by The Wu-Tang Clan**

Protecting your neck is also of UTMOST importance when it comes to your finances. We have spent a significant amount of time developing our Master Plan for our financial future. We learned about credit and now understand its uses and purpose, restored our credit as needed, developed a budget for today and tomorrow, acknowledged that Hard Times can affect everyone, and generated more income for ourselves through passive sources. If we continue along our Master Plan path, we will begin accumulating wealth and assets. That is a wonderful thing…until it is not! What good does it do us to gain wealth and assets and not protect them? Remember that we are all human and have a finite lifespan. As the old adage goes, "We can't take it with us." Also, sometimes "life" gets in the way and our situations may change causing the need for mutual protections to be in place. So what do we do? Do we just leave it in the bank and let the bank add our money into their enormous ledger? Do we allow the government to swoop in and gobble it all up? Or do we protect our legacy and develop procedures to protect our wealth? I don't know about you, but I couldn't care less about the bank's bottom line or the government when it comes to my family and their well-being.

PROTECTION FROM LAWSUITS

We must Protect Our Neck from all types of situations that may arise. One such situation is lawsuits. You have worked long and hard to create the type of portfolio that you can be proud of, yet you could lose it in an instant if you become a party to a lawsuit. Asset Protection is the concept and strategy for guarding your wealth. It is a legal insulation of your assets from creditors and legal matters. Whereas concealment of your assets is illegal, Asset Protection is not because it is done prior to any claim or liability occurring. Some common routes for Asset Protection include establishing asset protection trusts, accounts-receivable financing, and family limited partnerships (FLPs). An Asset Protection Trust is a trust established to safeguard assets from creditors and litigation. One thing to keep in mind is that only a handful of states actually allow an Asset Protection Trust. Accounts-receivable (A/R) financing is a fairly new phenomenon that shields your assets by obtaining a loan guaranteed by the A/R, purchasing a cash-value life insurance policy with the loan proceeds, and using the tax advantages associated with life insurance to create MORE cash values. Cash-value life insurance policies are used due to the fact that the cash invested inside the policy grows *tax-free* and come out *tax-free* via policy loans. Also, life insurance policies are protected from litigation in many states. A family limited partnership (FLP) is a partnership agreement that exists between family members that allows you to shift the value of assets to other members, thereby reducing the size of the estate for certain members and in some cases reducing the required estate taxes. Assets are transferred to the FLP and a general partner is assigned that will oversee the partnership. The partnership divides the rights to the income, assets, and control among the different family members, depending on the overall financial objective of the family. Although knowledgeable to the existence of ASP's, A/R financing, and FLP's, I am not an expert nor do I pretend to be. I would advise that you speak with an expert on the subject to determine which direction you should go.

You must also Protect Your Neck when it comes to insurances. This protection will include home insurance, car insurance, health insurance, and life insurance. As a habit, most people check the batteries in their smoke detectors on or around a specific date. It could be a birthday, an anniversary, or a holiday. Whatever the date, we are programmed to change our smoke detector batteries each year. We need to also get into the habit of checking our insurance policies. Do we have enough coverage on our insurances? Are we paying a fair amount for our insurances? Do we have unnecessary coverages on our policies? These are just a few quick things we need to check out. In today's times, it is something that can be done fairly easy. The incredible invention, that is the Internet, can help us search for alternatives for our policies. We must take into account all of the pros and cons to determine if it is prudent to stay as we are or switch to something different. Often times, people become comfortable with their insurance agents and will not want to change their policies. It's great to have a wonderful relationship with your agent; however, it is NOT wonderful to overpay for coverage or to be lacking in coverage just because you like someone. Business first, friends later. Make it a habit to comb through your policies. What good does it do you to have tsunami coverage when you live in Michigan? Or life insurance that does not cover the cost of burial? Or a brand new car without comprehensive and collision insurance? These are extremes, but something that needs to be monitored because it does happen.

Another area of protection that we must consider is retirement. Where will we live out the rest of our lives when we retire from working? Who is going to take care of us as we grow older? Will we have enough savings to pay for our golden years? These are the questions we must discuss NOW in order to develop our Golden Master Plan. This is a plan that is an extension of our Master Plan. Let's call it GMP. With all of the time and effort that we will be putting into our plan, a long and stress-free retirement should be our reward. Financially we should be set to retire, but in order to guarantee this stress-free living, we need to work on our GMP in coordination with our Master Plan. Hand in hand…Step by step. The end goal should always be for a stress-free senior living experience. We must develop a long-term care fund to help with our senior health needs, our senior living needs, and our senior care needs. This is a *Never-Going-To-Touch-Under-Any-Circumstances* fund. If you are like me, you love your children and do not want them to be saddled with the physical and financial burden of taking care of you, as you grow older.

PROTECT THE ESTATE

One of the most important and most uncomfortable financial protection that we need to consider is estate planning. I don't know one person that likes to think about estate planning. When you think about it, you have to come to grips with your own mortality. It becomes "REAL" when you begin to think and talk about life after your death. But it IS real! Just like taxes, it is a certainty. Get over your inhibitions and develop a plan for your estate now. The first step for estate planning is developing and SIGNING a will. It does no good to develop a will if you do not sign it. The purpose of the will is to make sure that your legacy remains with your family and not the government. You will decide which heir gets which assets to eliminate the possibility of fighting among family members after you are gone. You will also designate an executor to handle the execution of your will. This person will make sure that your wishes are carried out just as you designed them. Wills are a very important document to have prepared. That being said, statistically only 42 percent of adults in America have an executed will.[22] An alternative to a will is a revocable living trust that will pass assets to your heirs without the need for costly and time-consuming probate courts. If you have younger children, it is highly recommended to have a will to ensure the desire for guardianship in the event of an untimely death.

Step two of estate planning requires that you take a look at all of your accounts that have beneficiaries and make sure they are up to date and have the correct intended person listed. This will include bank and investment accounts, insurance policies, and retirement funds. Paul D. Hunt, an estate-planning lawyer in Alameda, CA, once asked a client why he had listed someone whom he had never mentioned during the planning process as the beneficiary of an account. Hunt recalls: "I called the client and he said, 'Oh, that's my brother. I haven't seen him in 26 years and since then, I've been married and had four kids, so we'd better change that.' "[23] This is not as uncommon as you may think. Just like the smoke detectors, remember to check your intended beneficiaries annually.

Step three of estate planning requires that you pay close attention to federal estate taxes. If you have to pay federal estate taxes, you are actually in a very good position. With the new laws, federal estate taxes are only due if you gift more than $5.25 million, increasing yearly with inflation…$10.5 million, if it is a husband and wife. But be careful. There are several states and the District of Columbia that have their own estate tax. If your estate is large enough to require paying estate taxes, I HIGHLY recommend that you contact a licensed estate planner as well as a tax lawyer to figure out your best course of action.

The next thing that you need to do is sit down and write a letter to your heirs. Yes, your will is designed to detail who gets what, but sometimes it is a great idea to tell them why. You can also include in your letter how you want your final arrangements to go. Did you desire a full funeral or just cremation? Do you want white doves released at the conclusion of your service? Maybe you want T. D. Jakes to deliver your eulogy. Whatever your desires, let it be known in your letter to your heirs. You may also have some sentimental items that you want them to have. Put it in the letter. This is a private letter written directly to them, without the legalese of a formal will. This personal touch can sometimes bring comfort during a time of sorrow and distress.

An additional requirement when developing your estate plan is to draw up a durable power of attorney (DPA). With a DPA, you designate someone that you want to take care of your affairs in the event that you cannot, due to health reasons or illness. If you do not have one, a judge will have to decide who can and should take care of the decisions as it pertains to your finances and your health. It is a much better idea for you to select a person to whom you are familiar and know will make the best decisions on your behalf, rather than have a judge, a complete stranger, decide between people he has very little or no idea of their character, motives, or knowledge of your wishes.

Step six requires that we develop an advanced healthcare directive. This is a plan of action in the event that you become gravely ill. It will let the hospital and doctors know the type of treatment you desire. This is accomplished by establishing both a DPA as well as a living will. The durable power of attorney for healthcare will acknowledge a healthcare agent that will make sure the doctors and other medical professionals carry out your healthcare wishes. A living will state the types of medical treatment you do or do not want. Due to HIPAA regulations, make sure your lawyer includes a clause in your living will and your DPA, to allow your healthcare agent to receive information about your health status and prescribed medical care.

Finally, step seven of your estate planning requires that you make hard copies as well as digital copies of all of your documents. Your estate executor will like you a lot more if you have all of your papers organized in both a binder and a digital file. Keep your original documents stored in a safe-deposit box, a home safe, or with your attorney. Organize any document that your executor may need for easy access, such as deed to burial plot, insurance policies, bank statements, investment statements, and pension and other employee-benefit information. Keep an up-to-date list of relevant phone numbers, current assets, account numbers and passwords, and inventory of safe-deposit box items. Make sure to keep all of this information as up to date as possible, to ensure everything still coincides with your wishes. Remember the smoke detector!

PROTECT YOUR LEGACY

Generational wealth, that's the key
My parents ain't have (jack), so that ship started with me
My mom took her money, she bought me bonds
That was the sweetest thing of all time, uh
Legacy, legacy, legacy, legacy
Black excellence baby, you gon' let 'em see
Legacy, legacy, legacy, legacy
Black excellency, baby, let 'em see

Legacy by Jay-Z

The concept of legacy teaches us to learn from our past, live for our present, and build for our future. Consider for a second a financial legacy. Did your parents leave you one? Are you creating one? Will your children build on what you started? These are some questions we need to ask ourselves. Susan Bosak of the Legacy Project asked the question: "Where do you think it is best to plant a young tree: a clearing in an old-growth forest or an open field?"[24] One would think a tree would grow better if it had more room to grow. That is not the case. The fact of the matter is that a young tree will grow better if it is planted in an area with older trees. But why is this true? Ecologists tell us that the roots of the young trees are able to follow along the paths created by the older trees and implant themselves deeper into the ground. Over the course of time, the roots of many trees may fuse together creating an "intricate, interdependent foundation" underground. This allows the stronger trees to share its resources with the weaker trees so that the forest, as a whole, becomes healthier. This is the best illustration of legacy I have ever heard. "An interconnection across time, with a need for those who have come before us and a responsibility to those who come after us." So what do we need to do in order to leave a financial legacy?

As with everything, education is the key. This includes building and maintaining a financial legacy. The first lesson you must learn is that it is never too late to begin developing a financial legacy. Even if your forefathers were not able to develop a financial legacy for you, it is abundantly important that you end the cycle and lay the first financial brick for future legacies. Brick one is your decision to actually begin. Now you must think about what exactly you want to leave for your descendants. This must line up with your other financial plans. Think about short-term plans and long-term plans and strategically start saving and investing towards the legacy you want to develop. But this part may be the most important: TALK WITH YOUR LOVED ONES. Keep open the lines of communication with the very ones for which you are developing the financial legacy. They must understand the lengths you are going to try to provide for them and their part in the whole plan. Teach them about credit, investments, and income sources. Teach them that the information is being passed to them in order for them to pass it on to their heirs. They need to understand the transfer of wealth is a very meaningful gift and how much it could mean for them today and their children tomorrow. Again this is legacy. Whether you are leaving a large inheritance or a small portfolio, passing along the values that you adhered to in order to build and sustain your wealth is the greatest gift. Give them hands-on experience working with money. In the Bible, Proverbs 22:6 says, "Train up a child in the way he should go: and when he is old, he will not depart from it." If you train them in the fundamentals of finances, they will develop interest and confidence in their money skills. One of the things you may try is opening an investment fund and allow them to completely manage the account...win or lose. Start them off with small amount and let them decide the fate of THEIR money. "What are we talking about? Practice? We're talkin' bout practice, man!" Yes, Allen Iverson said it correctly. We are indeed talking about practice. The more we teach our children to practice good financial principles, the better we are able to ensure that they will continue these practices as they grow older. Children who grow up to be good savers usually credit the parents that taught them to be good savers. The truth of the matter is that we have already started creating a financial legacy, be it first generation or tenth generation, when we developed our Master Plan and our Golden Plan. Now the time has come for us to impart this knowledge upon our children so that they will understand that the reason behind developing these plans is not just to be able to kick back when we retire, but the sacrifices made today are designed to make sure that generational wealth is developed, cultivated, and nurtured.

The reality is that we are all going to leave a legacy in one form or another, whether we like it or not. The extent of that legacy is up to us. We want to leave this legacy to show love to our heirs. Long after you are gone, your loved ones will know that you loved them by how well you prepared for their future. Your financial legacy will show love to your immediate family, your community, and your charitable causes. Your legacy will be used to provide a financial lift to those you love. Your financial legacy will allow your loved ones to possibly go further and faster than they otherwise could alone. Your sacrifice and discipline will go a long way in giving your future generations a head start towards debt-free living. That is a game-changing gift to your family tree. The habits that you pass down will leave lasting memories of your hard work and focus with your loved ones. Will your children pick up a dime that is on the ground? If you can answer this question in the affirmative, then you have successfully created a financial legacy.

> *And yeah, I'll be in a whole new tax bracket*
> *We in recession, but let me take a crack at it*
> *I'll probably take whatever's left and just split it up*
> *So everybody that I love can have a couple bucks*
> **Millionaire by Travie McCoy ft. Bruno Mars**

CHAPTER 6 HOT TAKES

1. We can't take it with us, so prepare a plan to protect your legacy and protect your wealth.

2. Protect your assets through asset protection trusts, accounts-receivable financing, and family limited partnerships.

3. Prepare your Estate Planning by following the seven steps.

4. Legacy teaches us to learn from our past, live for our present, and build for our future. The same can be said for Financial Legacy.

5. Education and training is key for establishing a Financial Legacy.

6. We will leave some kind of Financial Legacy, whether good or bad, whether we want to or not!

7. A financial legacy is a Game-Changing gift for our family.

THE
OUTRO

—

CHAPTER 7

CHAPTER 7 – THE OUTRO

I met this girl, when I was ten years old
And what I loved most she had so much soul
She was old school, when I was just a shorty
Never knew throughout my life she would be there for me

I Used To Love Her by Common

A s you may have probably suspected by now after reading this book, I am a big fan of Hip-Hop and all that it entails. I mean TRUE Hip-Hop…not this phony crap that you hear on the radio these days. I am a Real Fan; a fan of Run DMC, LL Cool J, EPMD, Biggie, Tupac, Jay-Z and so many of the earlier pioneers in the genre that paved the way for a movement to become a lifestyle. Hip-Hop and I have been through a lot! I am like Common in that she has always been there whenever I needed her. I could always call on a verse or a line in a Hip-Hop song to get me through many bad circumstances! When I was stressing over a young lady, I could look to Slick Rick and his **Teenage Love**, *"For the feelings were the same, now here's the score. You love him too much, and they don't love you anymore."* When doubt would ever creep into my mind, I would channel Pete Rock and CL Smooth

The Reminisce Over You, *"But only you saw what took many time to see, I dedicate this to you for believing in me."* And when faced with the most difficult time in my life, when my biggest cheerleader was called home to glory, Tupac reminded me *"All my childhood memories are full of all the sweet things you did for me."* (**Dear Mama**) The lyrics she gave you would resonate within your soul and cause emotions to stir up. The beats she gave you would cause your head to move and your body to sway. Not only do I USED to love her, I STILL do!!! Why? Because Hip-Hop can relate to ANY situation. She is the one true constant in an otherwise cold and chaotic world. One that will never leave you alone nor allow you to go through a situation without a word of encouragement. Okay that was a little much...but it sounded good, didn't it?! The truth of the matter is that Hip-Hop CAN relate to any situation.

We have spent our time together developing a plan to allow you to understand the importance of your credit history and protect it, to eliminate your debt by targeting your available income, to prevent future hard times by developing a plan to add more passive income, to build multiple sources of income using the passive income strategies, and to protect your developing financial legacy *BY ANY MEANS*

NECESSARY. This has been a great journey; one that I hope has allowed you to develop lasting generational wealth or at least develop an optimal plan to get you going in the right direction. If you have listened to a Christian church sermon, especially a Baptist church sermon, you will hear the pastor give you a passage of scripture and break down that scripture into a form that everyone can understand. No matter the topic, the pastor will explain it to you so that it moves your spirit and opens your eyes to a new understanding for something that you previously did not know or comprehend. After carefully breaking down the scriptures and getting the audience enthused about what was being spoken, the pastor would then close by telling everyone why they had come to church to hear the word in the first place, "Oh, but I know a MAN!!!"

My topic in this book is the painstaking process that you must endure to create a lasting financial legacy for your future generations. I have carefully broken down each topic to hopefully allow you to understand something that you did not previously know or understand. I pray that I have imparted a desire to want to do better financially for yourself and your family. I continue to pray that you have decided to develop your very own Master Plan and have become dedicated to the proposition of creating lasting generational wealth for you and your heirs. This journey together has been great. You have gone through a lot and you are much better because of your dedication and commitment. But just as the pastor only gives you a small portion of the Bible that he expounds upon, I am only giving you a small portion of the steps needed to completely fulfill your journey. More studying and more reading are needed to truly understand the subject. But do not fear, we both know you can do it! You have made it this far; let's continue to head towards that goal line! If you do not remember anything else from this book, remember that freedom is not free, especially financial freedom. Develop your plan, commit to your plan, and enact your plan. If you do these three things, your path to financial freedom will become a lot smoother.

But as I close, I want to tell you that when in doubt, SHE will always be there for you! Look to her for comfort. Use the lessons she has taught you as a guide.

If you havin' cash problems, I feel bad for you son.
I got 99 Problems But A Bill Ain't One!

I got the bills controlled and the money flows
Goals I that developed from the get-go.
Got critics that say boy your cash is low
They never seen my statements, what kind of facts is those?
I give you all the info so you also know
How to keep your score high and create the dough
Got 10 passive sources to bring the glow
To my face as my assets continue to grow.
Create a tight budget and work it for show
Cause I don't want hard times to knock at my door.
So I'll pay off my debt to keep the CREAM in tow
And protect my neck from folks trying to make me forgo
Creating a legacy, well that's just a no-go.
Cause I'm never satisfied with my current status quo.

I form my Master Plan bro cause I'm not dumb,
I Got 99 Problems But A Bill Ain't One!

(A Parady of 99 Problems by Jay-Z)

THE
APPENDIX

APPENDIX

THE APPENDIX

SAMPLE CREDIT REPORT (APPENDIX A)

Kroll Factual Data | **BUREAU** EXPRESS

Residential Merged Credit Report

KROLL FACTUAL DATA, 5200 HAHNS PEAK DRIVE LOVELAND, CO 80538 (800) 324-5005 OR FAX (800) 364-5005

BORROWERS NETWORK LLC	Client Tracking	Requested by	Report ID
2350 FRANKLIN RD STE 140	JOSEPH SAMPLE	Reva	72307BX0325100
BLOOMFIELD HILLS, MI 48302	Client Code	BX Date requested	Charges
(248)451-9588 (248)451-9566	2307-MI0623	11/01/2019 10:07:47	12.50

Identification (as requested)

	Applicant's last name		First name	Middle	Suffix	Age	Social Security
SAMPLE		JOSEPH					XXX-XX-9876

Residence Information (as requested)

Present	12345 MOCKINGBIRD LANE	ANYTOWN	MI	48187	Telephone

File Variations

Trans Union	BU1	XXX-XX-9876	JOSEPH SAMPLE	11/01/2019 10:08
Equifax	BQ1	XXX-XX-9876	JOSEPH SAMPLE	11/01/2019 10:08
Experian	BX1	XXX-XX-9876	JOSEPH SAMPLE	11/01/2019 10:08

Credit Score Information

	Repository	Brand	Type				
	Experian	Fair Isaac	FICO	XXX-XX-9876	SAMPLE, JOSEPH		BX1
727	038- Serious delinquency, and public record or collection filed						
	020- Length of time since derogatory public record or collection is too short						
	016- Lack of recent revolving account information						
	027- Too few accounts current paid as agreed						
	Repository	Brand	Type				
	Equifax	BEACON 5	FICO	XXX-XX-9876	SAMPLE, JOSEPH		BQ1
750	038- Serious delinquency, and public record or collection filed						
	020- Length of time since derogatory public record or collection is too short						
	016- Lack of recent revolving account information						
	014- Length of time accounts have been established						
	Repository	Brand	Type				
	TransUnion	Classic 04	FICO	XXX-XX-9876	SAMPLE, JOSEPH		BU1
712	038- Serious delinquency, and public record or collection filed						
	020- Length of time since derogatory public record or collection is too short						
	016- Lack of recent revolving account information						
	033- Proportion of current loan balance to original loan amount						

Credit History

	Opened	Reported	High balance	Reviewed	30	60	90+	Pastdue	Payment	Balance
LEXUS FINANCIAL	11/06	05/18	52,336	---	0	0	0			
0123456789	Last active 05/18	*BX1 *BU1 *BQ1 [Ind]	High limit		Install (I9)			-0-	Closed	-0-
	Closed Account, Paid In Full			Ratings: 05/18						

	Opened	Reported	High balance	Reviewed	30	60	90+	Pastdue	Payment	Balance
US DEPT ED	01/09	10/19	6,625	4 mos	0	0	0		120X $79	6,625
0123456789	Last active 10/19	*BX1 *BU1 *BQ1 [Ind]	High limit ---		Install (I9) Student loan			-0-		
	Student loan not in repayment; Payment deferred			Ratings: 10/19 1111111						

	Opened	Reported	High balance	Reviewed	30	60	90+	Pastdue	Payment	Balance
US DEPT OF EDUCATION	01/09	10/19	3,313	---	0	0	0		089X $ --	3,313
0123456789	Last active 10/19	*BX1 *BQ1 [Ind]	High limit ---		Install (I9) Student loan			-0-		

	Payment deferred			Ratings: 08/18 111						

	Opened 09/07	Reported 10/19	High balance 150	Reviewed ---	30 0	60 0	90+ 0	Pastdue -0-	Payment $15	Balance 350
PROVIDIAN FINANCIAL 0123456789	Last active 10/19	*BQ1 [Ind]	High limit 2500	Install (I9) Rev						
	Credit Card			Ratings: 10/19 111111111111111111111111						

	Opened 03/05	Reported 10/19	High balance 150	Reviewed ---	30 0	60 0	90+ 0	Pastdue -0-	Payment $20	Balance 150
TOTAL FIN 0123456789	Last active 10/19	*BU1 [Ind]	High limit 1500	Install (O9) Rev						
	Credit Card			Ratings: 10/19 111111111111111111111111						

	Opened 08/04	Reported 07/12	High balance 1,376	Reviewed ---	30 0	60 0	90+ 0	Pastdue -0-	Payment	Balance -0-
DTE ENERGY 0123456789	Last active 07/12	*BX1 *BU1 *BQ1 [Ind]	High limit 1,376	Install (I9) Unknown					06/12 Paid	
	Dte Energy Eft; Paid; DTE ENERGY EFT; Paid collection; Closed 06/10			Ratings: 07/12 1						

TOTALS	High credit	High balance			Pastdue	Payment	Balance
	2,376	11,614			0	0	10,438

Creditor Information

ALLIED INT (800)224-1797
3000 CORPORATE EXCHANGE DR., COLUMBUS, OH 43231
CAPITAL ONE BANK (804)934-2025
1500 CAPITAL ONE DRIVE, RICHMOND, VA 23285
CAPONEBANK
15000 CAPITAL ONE DRIVE PO#100794, RICHMOND, VA 23238
DTE ENERGY EFT (734)995-5360
6360 JACKSON ROAD SUITE #1, ANN ARBOR, MI 48103
FORD MOTOR CREDIT (602)667-0128
4050 E COTTON CENTER BLV, PHOENIX, AZ 85040

HSBC NV
2980 MEADE AVE STE A, LAS VEGAS, NV 89102
KROLL FACTUAL DATA/060 (970)663-5700
5200 HAHNS PEAK DR, LOVELAND, CO 80538
PROVIDIAN FINANCIAL (800) 356-0011
PO BOX 660509, DALLAS, TX 75266-0509
US DEPT ED
PO BOX 7202 UTICA, NY 13504-7202

Public Records

No Public Records found

Inquiry Information

NONE FOUND

TruAlert - Applicant

SocialID

SSN Validation	Deceased Flag	Potential DOB found
SSN XXX-XX-9876 was issued in Michigan	SSN XXX-XX-9876 has not been reported as deceased	No information found
Recent Change of Address found	FKA / AKA Records found	
No information found.	None found.	

SSN	Name	Address
XXX-XX-9876	SAMPLE, JOSEPH	12345 MOCKINGBIRD LANE, ANYTOWN, MI 48187

XXX-XX-9876	SAMPLE, JOSEPH	12345 MOCKINGBIRD LANE, ANYTOWN, MI 48187

OFAC Compliance

Applicant input name checked. No similar records found in OFAC's SDN list.

File Variations

No additional File Variation names found.

AKA Records

AKA records checked. No similar records found in OFAC's SDN list.

IDScan

SNID SEARCH: SS# XXX-XX-9876 ISSUED 1956-1989 STATE: Michigan

Research Results:

THE APPLICANT'S INPUT SOCIAL SECURITY NUMBER LISTS MULTIPLE IDENTITIES. PLEASE REVIEW THE TRACE REPORT AND VERIFY THAT ALL OF THE IDENTITIES BELONG TO YOUR APPLICANT. IF THE IDENTITIES DO BELONG TO YOUR APPLICANT, REVIEW THE FILE SEGMENTS TO DETERMINE WHICH IDS ARE NOT INCLUDED AND RESUBMIT A CORRECTED REQUEST TO ENSURE AN ACCURATE SEARCH OF THE REPOSITORIES DATABASES.

The TruAlert products (RiskID and SocialID) cannot be used as factors in establishing a customer's eligibility for credit, residence, or employment.

AKA

AKA: **SAMPLE, JOSEPH**   BU1

Comments

TransUnion Alert: Record inquiries alert: 0 inquiry has been made in the last 60 days.

BU1

Fraud Search

FACTA: Address mismatch alert - The current input address does not match the file address.

TransUnion Hawk Alert was completed on applicant by searching applicant s name, social security number and address. No fraudulent activity was found.

BU1

FACTA: Address mismatch Alert - The address submitted in the inquiry is substantially different from the address on file.

BQ1

FACTA: Address mismatch alert: Input address did not match the best address on file.

BX1

Database Employment Information

Database Employment Information		First	Last	
GLOBAL SERVICES		04/91	---	BQ1

Database Residence Information

Database Residence Information				First	Last	
17150 CANTON	ANYCITY	MI	48235	---	09/08	BU1

Information Sources

This report includes information retrieved from the following repository(ies):

TransUnion Consumer Relations	Equifax Consumer Relations	Experian Consumer Relations
PO Box 1000	PO Box 740241	PO Box 2002
Chester, PA 19022	Atlanta, GA 30374	Allen, TX 75013
(800) 888-4213	(800) 685-1111	(888) 397-3742

SAMPLE DISPUTE LETTER (APPENDIX B)

Joe Sample
12345 Mockingbird Lane
Anytown, MI 48187
SSN: 000-00-0000 | DOB: 7/1/19XX

October 24, 20XX

Equifax
P.O. Box 740256
Atlanta, GA 30374

This letter is to inform you that I recently received a copy of my credit report that your company publishes and after reviewing it I found a number of items on the report that are inaccurate. The accounts in question are listed below.

Please send me copies of the documents that you have in your files as of this date that you used to verify the accuracy of the accounts listed below.

Under the Fair Credit Reporting Act, **15 U.S.C. § 1681g** I have the right to demand that you disclose to me all of the documents that you have recorded and retained in your file at the time of this request concerning the accounts that you are reporting in my credit report. Please don't respond to my request by saying that these accounts have been verified. Send me copies of the documents that you have in your files that were used to verify them.

If you do not have any documentation in your files to verify the accuracy of these disputed accounts then please delete them immediately as required under **Section 611(a)(5)(A)(i)**. By publishing these inaccurate and unverified items on my credit report and distributing them to 3rd parties you are damaging my reputation and credit worthiness.

Under the FCRA 15 U.S.C. § 1681i, all unverified accounts must be promptly deleted. Therefore, if you are unable to provide me with a copy of the verifiable proof that you have on file for each of the accounts listed below within 30 days of receipt of this letter then you must remove these accounts from my credit report.

Please provide me with a copy of an updated and corrected credit report showing these items removed.

I demand the following accounts be properly verified or removed immediately:
(*Hand Write this information with blue ink pen. Provide Physical Proof of Verification*)

Name of Account:	Account Number:	
1. Chase Bank	#533376304023 ...	Unverified Account
2. Chase Bank	#533376304023 ...	Unverified Account
3. Chase Bank	#533376304023 ...	Unverified Account
4. Chase Bank	#533376304023 ...	Unverified Account
5. Chase Bank	#533376304023 ...	Unverified Account

(Make sure that you don't have more than 5 accounts listed on each letter. If more accounts need to be disputed, send out multiple letters, but space them at least 14 days apart.)

* NOTE: Please also remove all non-account holding inquiries over 30 days old.

Thank You,

Sign your name here

(Your Name Here)

<u>Attached</u>: Copy of my Social Security Card & Drivers License is attached
Sent: USPS Certified Mail

Take these cards down to your copy center and make clear copies of both on one sheet.
They must be legible or else the credit bureaus will reject them.

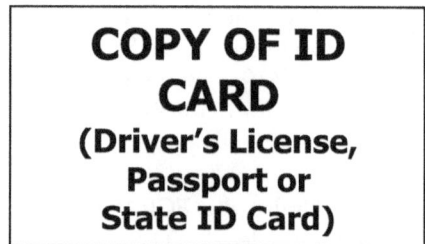

COPY of SSN CARD

COPY OF ID CARD **(Driver's License, Passport or State ID Card)**

CREDIT BUREAU CONTACT INFORMATION

(APPENDIX C)

EQUIFAX	*EXPERIAN*	*TRANS UNION*
P.O. Box 740256	P.O. Box 2002	P.O. Box 2000
Atlanta, GA 30374	Allen, TX 75013	Chester, PA 19022
(888) 548-7878	**(888) 397-3742**	**(800) 916-8800**
www.equifax.com	www.experian.com	www.transunion.com

SAMPLE DEBT VALIDATION & 609 LETTERS

(APPENDIX D)

Date: October 24, 20XX

Joe Sample
12345 Mockingbird Lane
Anytown, MI 48187

Midwest Recovery Systems
2747 W Clay St A
Saint Charles, MO 63301

RE: Account # XXXXXXXX

To Whom It May Concern:

Be advised this is not a refusal to pay, but a notice that your claim is disputed and validation is requested. Under the *Fair Debt collection Practices Act (FDCPA)*, I have the right to request validation of the debt you say I owe you. I am requesting proof that I am indeed the party you are asking to pay this debt, and there is some contractual obligation that is binding on me to pay this debt.

This is NOT a request for "verification" or proof of my mailing address, but a request for VALIDATION made pursuant to 15 USC 1692g Sec. 809 (b) of the FDCPA. I respectfully request that your offices provide me with competent evidence that I have any legal obligation to pay you.

At this time I will also inform you that if your offices have or continue to report invalidated information to any of the three major credit bureaus (Equifax, Experian, Trans Union), this action might constitute fraud under both federal and state laws. Due to this fact, if any negative mark is found or continues to report on any of my credit reports by your company or the company you represent, I will not hesitate in bringing legal action against you and your client for the following: Violation of the Fair Debt Collection Practices Act *and* Defamation of Character.

My attorney and your legal staff will agree that non-compliance with this request could put your company in serious legal trouble with the FTC and other state or federal agencies.

If your offices are able to provide the proper documentation as requested in the following declaration, I will require 30 days to investigate this information and during such time all collection activity must cease and desist. Also, during this validation period, if any action is taken which could be considered detrimental to any of my credit reports, I will consult with my firm's managing attorney for suit. This includes any listing of any information to a credit-reporting repository that could be inaccurate or invalidated. If your offices fail to respond to this validation request within 30 days from the date of your receipt, all references to this account must be deleted and completely removed from my credit file and a copy of such deletion request shall be sent to me immediately. It would be advisable that you and your client assure that your records are in order before I am forced to take legal action.

CREDITOR/DEBT COLLECTOR DECLARATION

Please provide the following:

- Agreement with your client that grants you the authority to collect on this alleged debt.
- Agreement that bears the signature of the alleged debtor wherein he/she agreed to pay the creditor.
- Any insurance claims been made by any creditor regarding this account.
- Any Judgments obtained by any creditor regarding this account.
- Name and address of alleged creditor.
- Name on file of alleged debtor.
- Alleged account number.
- Address on file for alleged debtor.
- Amount of alleged debt.
- Date this alleged debt became payable.
- Date of original charge off or delinquency.
- Verification that this debt was assigned or sold to collector.
- Complete accounting of alleged debt.
- Commission for debt collector if collection efforts are successful.

Please provide the name and address of the bonding agent for <<ENTER NAME OF COLLECTION AGENCY>> in case legal action becomes necessary. Your claim cannot and WILL NOT be considered if any portion of the above is not completed and returned with copies of all requested documents. This is a request for validation made pursuant to the Fair Debt Collection Practices Act. Please allow 30 days for processing after I receive this information back.

Best Regards
SIGN YOUR NAME HERE

[ENTER YOUR NAME HERE]
cc: Federal Trade Commission

609 Letter

Joe Sample
12345 Mockingbird Lane
Anytown, MI 48187
SSN: 000-00-0000 | DOB: 7/1/19XX

October 24, 20XX

Equifax
P.O. Box 740256
Atlanta, GA 30374

This letter is to inform you that I recently received a copy of my credit report that your company publishes and after reviewing it I found a number of items on the report that are inaccurate. The accounts in question are listed below. Please send me copies of the documents that you have in your files as of this date that you used to verify the accuracy of the accounts listed below.

Under the Fair Credit Reporting Act, 15 U.S.C. § 1681g I have the right to demand that you disclose to me all of the documents that you have recorded and retained in your file at the time of this request concerning the accounts that you are reporting in my credit report. Please don't respond to my request by saying that these accounts have been verified. Send me copies of the documents that you have in your files that were used to verify them. If you do not have any documentation in your files to verify the accuracy of these disputed accounts then please delete them immediately as required under Section 611(a)(5)(A)(i). By publishing these inaccurate and unverified items on my credit report and distributing them to 3rd parties you are damaging my reputation and credit worthiness.

Under the FCRA 15 U.S.C. § 1681i, all unverified accounts must be promptly deleted. Therefore, if you are unable to provide me with a copy of the verifiable proof that you have on file for each of the accounts listed below within 30 days of receipt of this letter then you must remove these accounts from my credit report.

Please provide me with a copy of an updated and corrected credit report showing these items removed, I demand the following accounts be properly verified or removed immediately.

*(**Hand Write** this information with **_blue_** ink pen. **_Provide Physical Proof of Verification_**)*

Name of Account:	Account Number:	
1. Chase Bank	#533376304023 ...	Unverified Account
2. Chase Bank	#533376304023 ...	Unverified Account
3. Chase Bank	#533376304023 ...	Unverified Account
4. Chase Bank	#533376304023 ...	Unverified Account
5. Chase Bank	#533376304023 ...	Unverified Account

(Make sure that you don't have more than 5 accounts listed on each letter. If more accounts need to be disputed, send out multiple letters, but space them at least 14 days apart.)

* NOTE: Please also remove all non-account holding inquiries over 30 days old.

Thank You,
Sign your name here
(Your Name Here)

Attach: Copy of your Social Security Card & Driver's License
Send: USPS Certified Mail

COPY of SSN CARD

COPY OF ID CARD
(Driver's License, Passport or State ID Card)

SAMPLE PAY FOR DELETION LETTER

(APPENDIX E)

Joe Sample
12345 Mockingbird Lane
Anytown, MI 48187

Midwest Recovery Systems
2747 W Clay St A
Saint Charles, MO 63301

October 24, 20XX
Re: Account Number XXXX-XXXX-XXXX-XXXX

Dear Collection Specialist:

I am writing this letter in response to your recent correspondence related to the account number I referenced in the subject line above. I am considering the possibility of settling this debt.

I accept no responsibility for ownership of this debt. However, I'm willing to compromise. I can offer a significant settlement amount in exchange for the following:

1.   You agree, in writing, to designate the account as "payment in full" once you are in receipt of the agreed upon payment amount. The account will not be designated as a "paid collection" or "settled account."
2.   You agree, in writing, to completely remove any and all references to this account from all credit bureaus to which you report.

I am willing to pay the <full balance owed / $XXX as settlement for this debt> in exchange for your agreement to remove all information regarding this debt from all credit reporting agencies to which you report within fifteen calendar days of receipt of payment.

When I am in receipt of a signed agreement with the aforementioned terms from an authorized representative on your company letterhead, I will pay $XXX via <cashier's check/wire transfer/money order>.

If I do not receive your response to this offer within fifteen calendar days, I will rescind this offer and follow up with a method of verification letter.

THE APPENDIX

Please forward your agreement to the address listed above at your earliest convenience, as I look forward to resolving this matter quickly.

Sincerely,

Your Name

AFTER-TAX EXPENSE WORKSHEET
(APPENDIX F)

AFTER-TAX EXPENSE WORKSHEET

AFTER-TAX MONTHLY INCOME		$
FIXED EXPENSES		
	$	
	$	
	$	
	$	
	$	
	$	
	$	
	$	
TOTAL FIXED EXPENSES		$
VARIABLE EXPENSES		
	$	
	$	
	$	
	$	
	$	
	$	
	$	
	$	
	$	
	$	
	$	
TOTAL VARIABLE EXPENSES		$
AFTER-TAX INCOME MINUS EXPENSES		$

REFERENCES

—

WORK CITED

REFERENCES

1. "Problem: Meaning of Problem by Lexico." *Lexico Dictionaries | English*, Lexico Dictionaries, www.lexico.com/definition/problem.

2. Holland, Kelley. "Fighting with Your Spouse? It's Probably about This." *CNBC*, CNBC, 4 Feb. 2015, www.cnbc.com/2015/02/04/money-is-the-leading-cause-of-stress-in-relationships.html.

3. *American Psychological Association*, American Psychological Association, www.apa.org/news/press/releases/2015/02/money-stress.

4. *Board of Governors of the Federal Reserve System*, 2018, 4. https://www.federalreserve.gov/publications/files/2017-report-economic-well-being-us-households-201805.pdf.

5. Taylor, Jane. "20 Inspiring Quotes from Lao Tzu." *Jane Taylor | Re-Alignment Coach | Accountability Coach | Wellbeing Coaching | Mindful Self-Compassion Coaching | Gold Coast | Mindfulness Teacher*, 2013, www.habitsforwellbeing.com/20-inspiring-quotes-from-lao-tzu.

REFERENCES

6. Leibowitz, Jon. "Section 319 of the Fair and Accurate Credit Transactions Act of 2003: Fifth Interim Federal Trade Commission Report to Congress Concerning the Accuracy of Information in Credit Reports (December 2012) 1 / 370." *Https://Www.ftc.gov/*, Federal Trade Commission, 2012, www.ftc.gov/sites/default/files/documents/reports/section-319-fair-and-accurate-credit-transactions-act-2003-fifth-interim-federal-trade-commission/130211factareport.pdf.

7. "State Court Caseload Statistics." *Bureau of Justice Statistics (BJS)*, 2012, www.bjs.gov/index.cfm?ty=tp&tid=30.

8. Jolley, Willie. "Today's 'Live Better With Willie Jolley' Tip: Your Dreams Can Change The World." *Live Better with Dr. Willie Jolley*, 15 Apr. 2010, williejolley.wordpress.com/2010/04/15/today%E2%80%99s-%E2%80%98live-better-with-willie-jolley%E2%80%99-tip-your-dreams-can-change-the-world/.

9. "Master plan." *The Merriam-Webster.com Dictionary*, Merriam-Webster Inc., https://www.merriam-webster.com/dictionary/master%20plan. Accessed 5 January 2020.

10. "A Quote by Maya Angelou." *Goodreads*, Goodreads, 2015, www.goodreads.com/quotes/7273813-do-the-best-you-can-until-you-know-better-then.

11. "Gail Devers Quotes." *BrainyQuote*, Xplore, www.brainyquote.com/quotes/gail_devers_144884.

12. Fay, Bill. "The U.S. Consumer Debt Crisis." *Debt.org*, www.debt.org/faqs/americans-in-debt/.

13. "Process: Definition of Process by Lexico." *Lexico Dictionaries | English*, Lexico Dictionaries, www.lexico.com/en/definition/process.

14. Dilworth, Kelley. "'Jamming' Cleans Your Credit -- Temporarily." *Yahoo! Finance*, Yahoo!, 20 Feb. 2014, finance.yahoo.com/news/jamming-cleans-credit-temporarily-130000766.html?guccounter=1&guce_referrer=aHR0cHM6Ly93d3cuZ29vZ2xlLmNvbS88&guce_referrer_sig=AQAA ACCT1x9e4-oguCi73stWw4x-OXGcJEiss9U1CJS3rBAS0g-N1PgjSijwc1brfa7A2KQ7FMrHTAcTUJcgEKtIMaaK2s-ZVHGOed-8n7EWY_7XSyW7HN1_W8QOEr-Hy6LsK3kSIYNNB0tGREybSxwxcbPFydDKx-cECxuCnj8AvhNZ.

15. Dickens, Charles. *A Tale of Two Cities*. Klopp, 1947.

16.   "Personal Income in the United States." *Wikipedia*,
        Wikimedia Foundation, 3 Dec. 2019,
        en.m.wikipedia.org/wiki/Personal_income_in_the_United_
        States.

17.   "Average American Carrying $15K in Credit Card Debt:
        NerdWallet." *AccountsRecovery.net*, 12 Dec. 2017,
        www.accountsrecovery.net/2017/12/12/average-american-
        carrying-15k-credit-card-debt-nerdwallet/.

18.   Friedman, Zack. "Student Loan Debt Statistics In 2018: A
        $1.5 Trillion Crisis." *Forbes*, Forbes Magazine, 14 Oct.
        2019,
        www.forbes.com/sites/zackfriedman/2018/06/13/student-
        loan-debt-statistics-2018/#462d81c67310.

19.   Haltiwanger, John. "5 Quotes From Bill Gates That Prove
        You Need To Fail To Succeed." *Elite Daily*, 10 Oct. 2014,
        www.elitedaily.com/money/bill-gates-quotes-on-sucess-and-
        failure/791158.

20.   Publishing, Corsair's. "The Martian - Lessons in Problem
        Solving." *Medium*, Creative Analytics, 29 Nov. 2016,
        creative-analytics.corsairs.network/the-martian-lessons-in-
        problem-solving-e4cf4f613ccf.

21.   "2014 Individual Income Tax Returns Complete Report
        Now Available: Internal Revenue Service." *2014 Individual
        Income Tax Returns Complete Report Now Available |
        Internal Revenue Service*, 31 Aug. 2016,
        www.irs.gov/newsroom/2014-individual-income-tax-
        returns-complete-report-now-available.

22.   "More Than Half of American Adults Don't Have a Will,
        2017 Survey Shows." *Caring.com*, 2018,
        www.caring.com/caregivers/estate-planning/wills-
        survey/2017-survey/.

23.   "Steps to Create an Estate Plan - Consumer Reports." *Steps
        to Create an Estate Plan - Consumer Reports*, Nov. 2013,
        www.consumerreports.org/cro/2013/11/how-to-create-a-
        bulletproof-estate-plan/index.htm.

24.   Bosak, Susan. "What Is Legacy?" *What Is Legacy?*,
        www.legacyproject.org/guides/whatislegacy.html.

REFERENCES

www.ingramcontent.com/pod-product-compliance
Lightning Source LLC
Chambersburg PA
CBHW021144090426
42740CB00008B/934